# Tiny Wardrobe

12 adorable designs and patterns for your doll

HANON
-SATOMI FUJII-

## contents

This is a book of sewing patterns for doll-size clothes.
The simply formed items have been carefully designed to create perfect silhouettes and these sewing patterns have been written with beginners in mind.

With plenty of lace, modern, stylish muted colors along with cute pastel shades and more, you can add your own special touches and enjoy trying out different seasonal fabrics and techniques.

These clothes have been designed to fit the following sizes:
S size is for Middie Blythe dolls
M size is for Neo Blythe dolls, and
L size is for Unoa 1.5 Girls.
They may well suit other dolls of a similar size.
Give them a try!

M size Embroidered Smock Dress, Waist Apron, Lace Strap Dress and Boots

Enjoy making matching items in S and M sizes.
The designs have been created so that rather than just reducing the sizes,
the volumes and lengths of fabric have been adjusted to fit each doll.

M size Lace Strap Dress and Sarouel Pants

M size Peter Pan Collar Dress and Socks

POLSKA
ČESKÁ REPUBLIKA
posta romana

M size Blouse, Skirt, Socks and Boots

M size Linen Coat and Boots

Change the whole appearance of the outfit by using different materials.
Strips of leather and ribbon can be wrapped as belts and embroidery added
to create your very own fashion style.

Tiny Betsy McCall looks good in both S and M size items.
Why not try making a whole wardrobe of clothes for her to wear?

S size Peter Pan Collar Dress, Shoulder Bag, M size Boots and Socks

S size Embroidered Smock Dress, Sarouel Pants and M size Boots

M size is a little long for Betsy.
Adjust the length for her as you like.

**M size Lace Strap Dress, Corsage and Cheeky Fox**

M size short Embroidered Smock Dress, M size Skirt and Boots

Some of the M size items can fit the slender 1/6 Unoa Quluts Light dolls.
They will be short though, so it is recommended to alter the length to one you like.

**M size Embroidered Smock Dress and Sarouel Pants**

M size Blouse, Waistcoat, Trousers, Socks and Boots

L size Blouse, Waistcoat, Trousers and Boots

L size can be worn by Unoa Quluts Girls in both bust sizes.
The dresses and other items with loose silhouettes may fit other 40 cm (16 in) dolls too.

L size Embroidered Smock Dress, Lace Strap Dress and Sarouel Pants

L size Lace Strap Dress, Sarouel Pants and Boots

L size Coat, Skirt and Boots

L size Peter Pan Collar Dress, Waist Apron, Socks and Boots

L size Embroidered Smock Dress, Lace Strap Dress and Boots

These items have been designed with a loose fit for easy wearing,
so items like coats and waistcoats can be layered. Enjoy trying out a range of styles.

L size Peter Pan Collar Dress, Waistcoat, Corsage and Shoulder Bag

# Tools

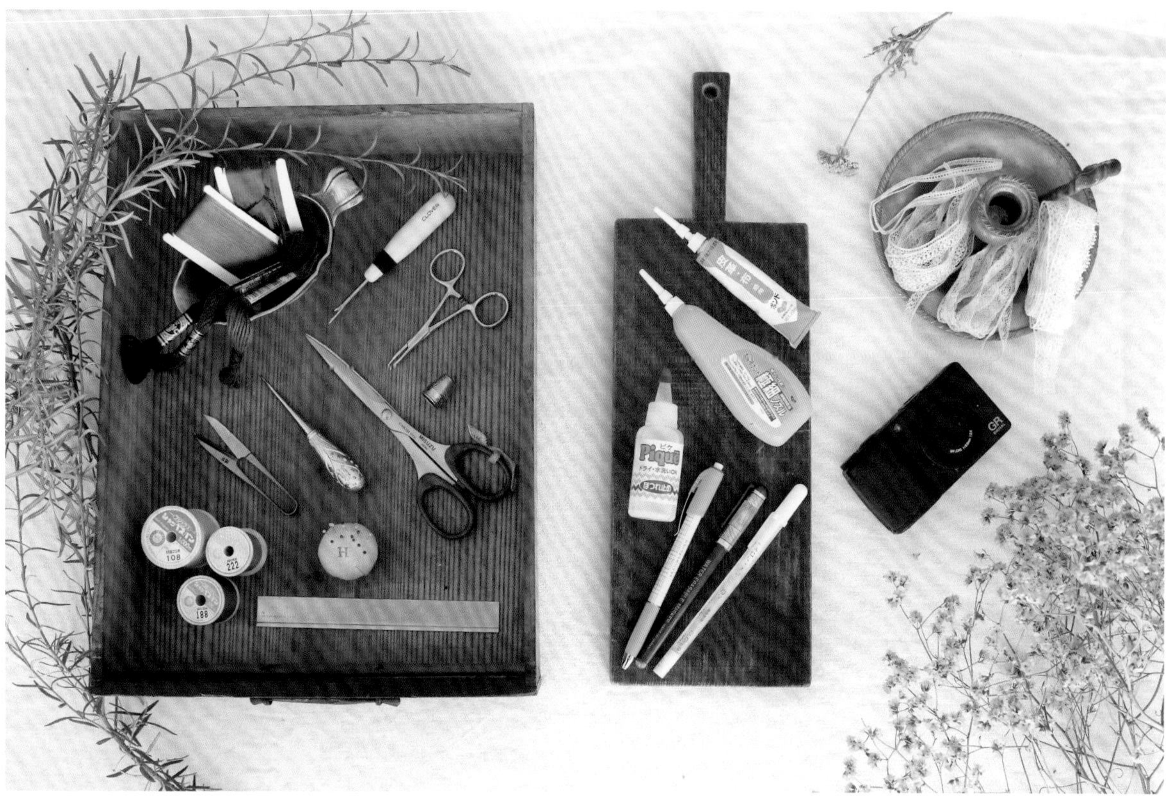

Before beginning to make these doll clothes, make sure you have all the tools you need. Tools that might not normally be used in sewing can be very useful when making small doll clothes.

**Silk Embroidery Ribbon**

Ribbons measuring 3.5 mm (0.14 in), used for ribbon embroidery, are supple and easy to use, and come in a wide choice of colors.

**Cotton Embroidery Floss**

I normally use one strand of DMC size 25 embroidery floss.

**Seam Ripper**

Handy for cleanly cutting the thread when fixing seams that are not straight.

**Tweezers**

Small tweezers make it very easy to turn the tiny fabric pieces the right side out.

**Thread Scissors**

For cutting the ends of hand sewing and machine threads.

**Thimble**

Used when embroidering pieces or doing blind stitches.

**Tailor's Awl**

Used for pushing the corners out when turning fabric pieces the right side out and holding fabric in place when sewing by machine.

**Dressmaking Scissors**

Choose a small pair that cut cleanly and can be used for intricate work. I use Misuzu Quilt Cut scissors.

**Sewing Thread**

I love using Fujix Schappe Spun #90 thread for both machine and hand sewing.

**Fabric Glue**

I recommend Kawaguchi fabric glue that can be used for leather, fabric, and paper, and which becomes transparent when hardened. The slender nozzle makes it easy to apply glue to small areas.

**Fray Stopper Liquid**

My favorite is Kawaguchi Pique fray stopper liquid. After cutting the fabric, apply this to the edges to stop them fraying.

**Tailor's Chalk**

I use Charisma (Sewline) Fabric Pencil for thin fabric, Chacopaper Fine Tip Marker for thick fabric like corduroy, and Clover White Marking Pen for dark-colored fabric.

**Assorted Lace Trim**

Vintage lace is shown on this page. New lace can look too bright and not match the fabric, so try dyeing it naturally with plants or black tea to create a more suitable color.

**Snaps and Hooks**

I use 5 mm (0.2 in) round snap fasteners and 0 size hook-and-eye closures.

**Sewing Needles, Marking Pins, Silk Pins, Ruler**

# Lace Strap Dress

This dress, embellished with lace remnants, is good for beginners.
The shoulder straps allow the length to be adjusted, so it can be paired with other items.

| | | |
|---|---|---|
| Cotton voile | S | 30 × 20 cm (11.8 × 7.9 in) |
| | M | 42 × 25 cm (16.5 × 9.8 in) |
| | L | 93 × 45 cm (36.6 × 17.7 in) |
| 5 mm (0.2 in) lace | S | 12 cm (4.7 in) × 2 strips |
| | M | 14 cm (5.5 in) × 2 strips |
| | L | 19 cm (7.5 in) × 2 strips |

| | | |
|---|---|---|
| Skirt lace [Approx. 7–10 cm (2.8–3.9 in)] | S | 13 + 4 cm (5.1 + 1.6 in) |
| | M | 20 + 7 cm (7.9 + 2.8 in) |
| | L | 45 + 12 cm (17.7 + 4.7 in) |
| Lace scraps | | Enough to cover the bodice section |
| Snaps | | S, M 1 pair L 2 pairs |

1

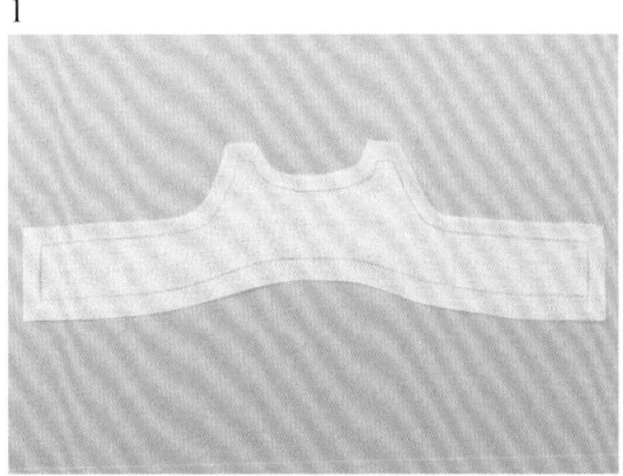

Arrange the paper templates on the fabric and cut out all the sections, then apply fray stopper liquid to all the edges.

2

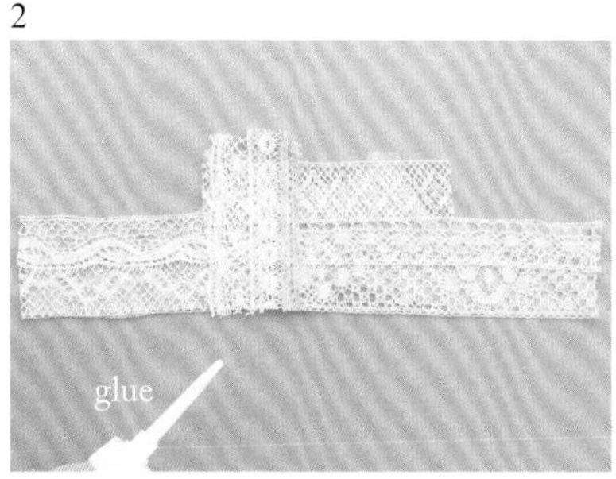


Place lace scraps on the front bodice section and temporarily fix them with fabric glue.

3

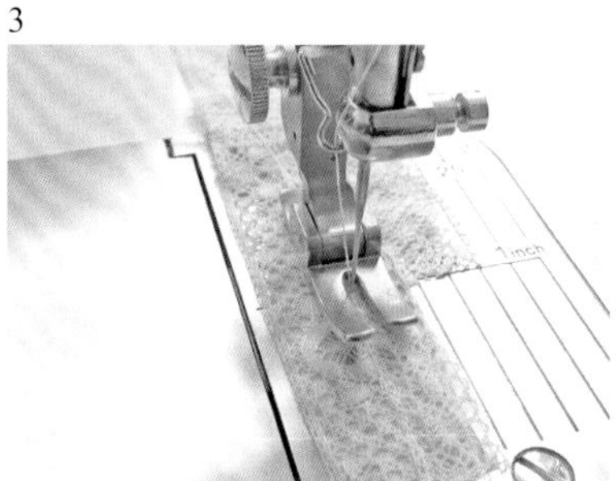

Sew the edges of the lace and then sew it on to the bodice.

4

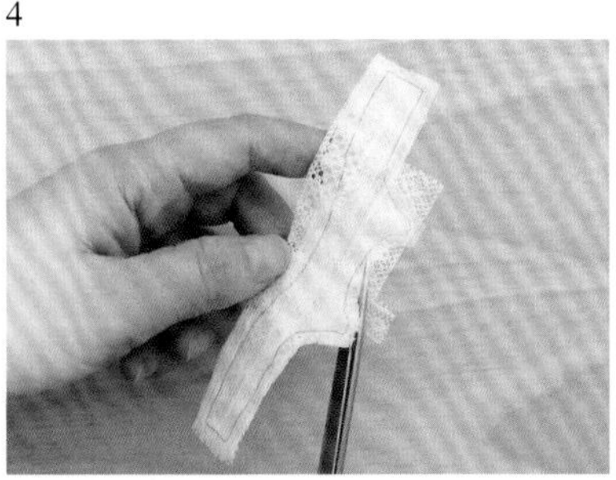

Cut any lace that protrudes out from the bodice. For sizes S and M, go straight to step 7.

5

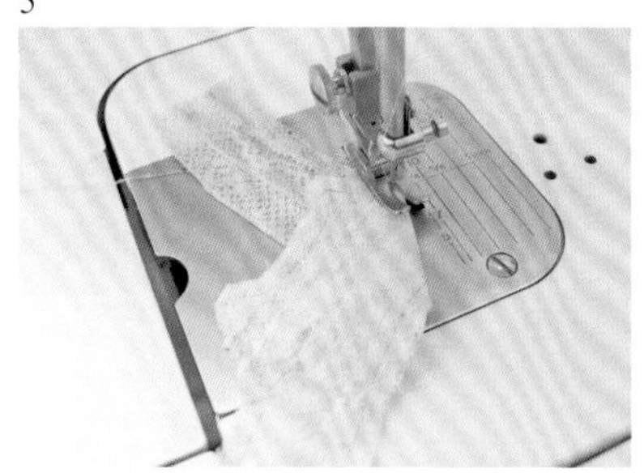

For size L only, fold the mid-armhole darts on the bodice in half, right sides together, and sew them.

6

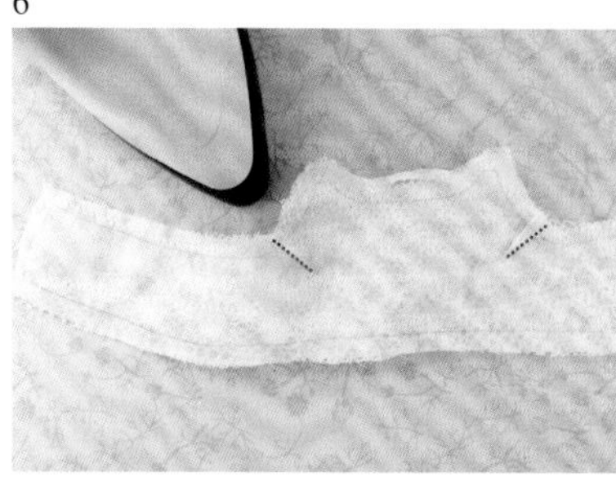

For size L only, fold the darts inwards and iron them flat.

7

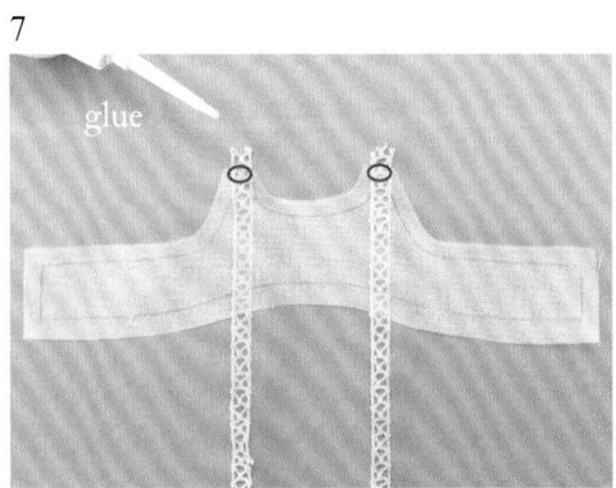


Create the lace straps for the dress by temporarily attaching 5 mm (0.2 in) lace to the shoulders of the back bodice section with a small amount of fabric glue.

8

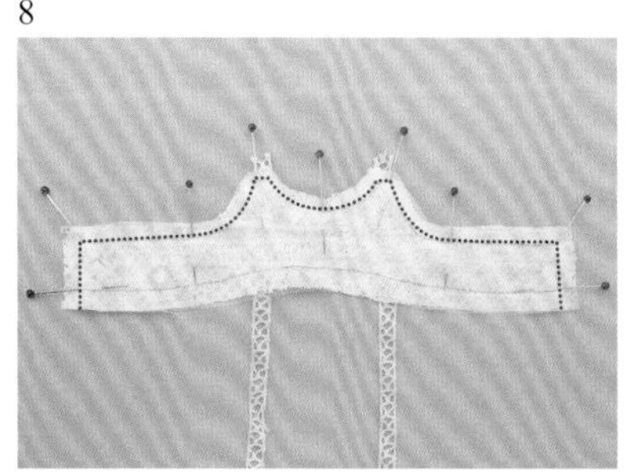

Align the front and back bodice sections so they are inside out and, leaving the waist part open, sew the sides.

9

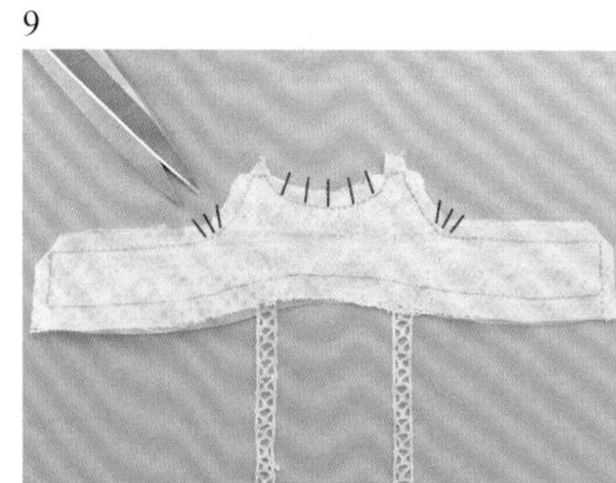

Cut the corners of the seam allowances, cutting fine slits where the fabric curves. Be careful not to cut the stitches.

10

Turn the piece the right side out, using a tailor's awl to neatly push out the corners and curves, then iron into shape.

11

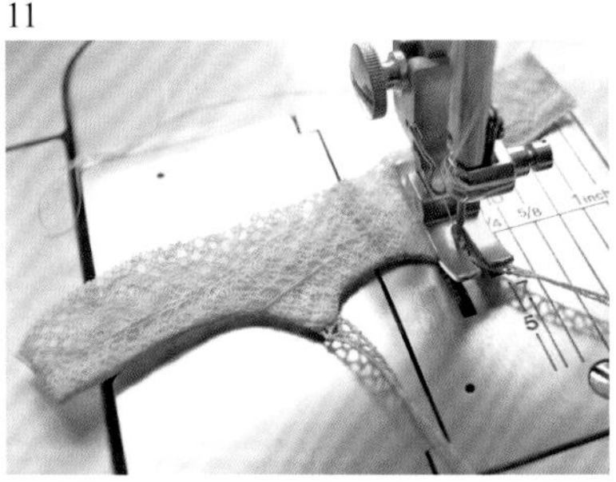

Leaving the waist part open, press down and sew around the edges.

12

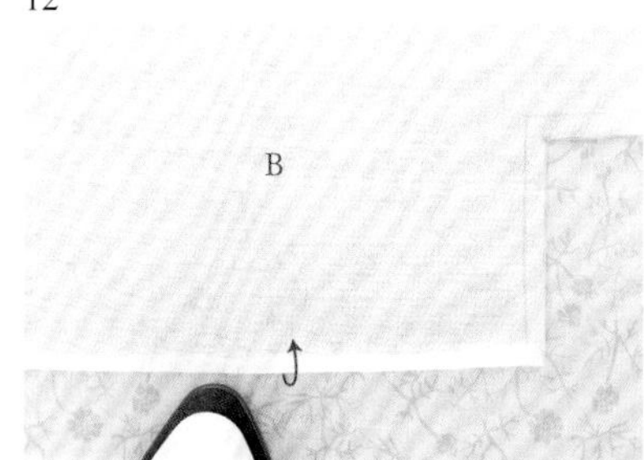


Fold the lower hem of the Skirt B section inwards and sew.

13

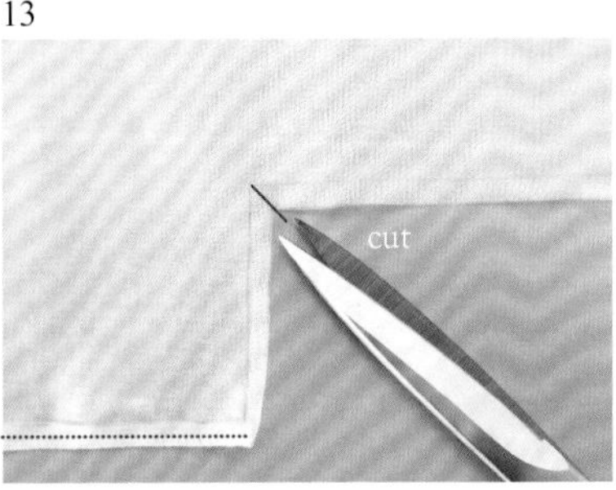


Cut slits into the corners of Skirt B's upper hem.

14

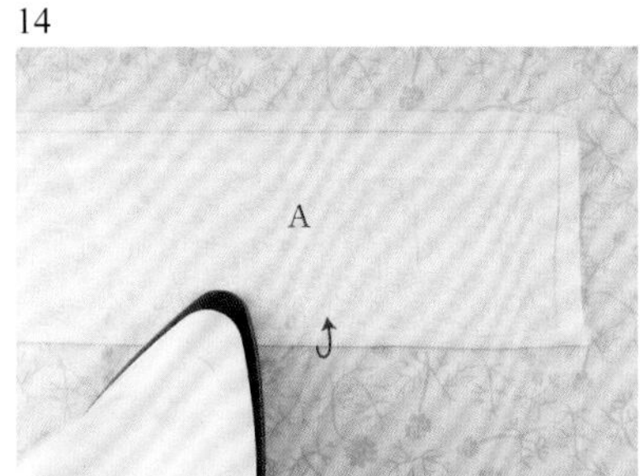


Fold the seam allowance of Skirt A's hem inwards and sew.

15

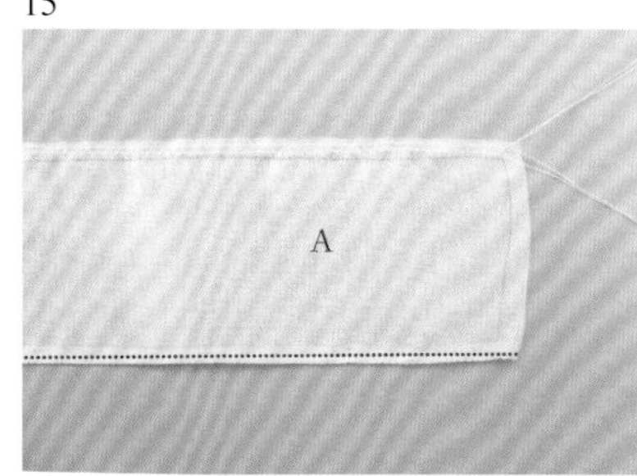


Use a machine to sew gathering stitches in the upper seam allowance of Skirt A. Make the stitch length 2.5 mm (0.1 in) and sew two lines on the seam allowance.

16

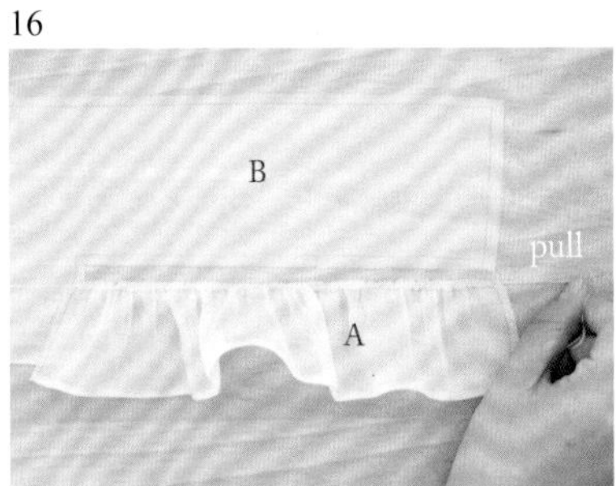


Align with the width of the upper hem of Skirt B (where Section A will be inserted) and gather the fabric (refer to p. 92).

17

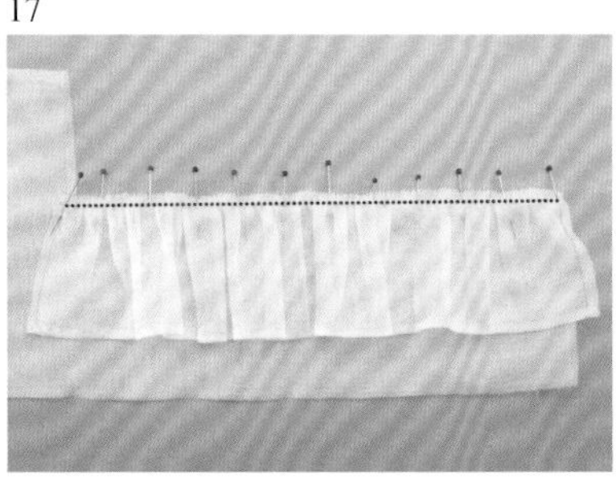

With right sides facing, align the gathered Skirt A with B and sew together.

18

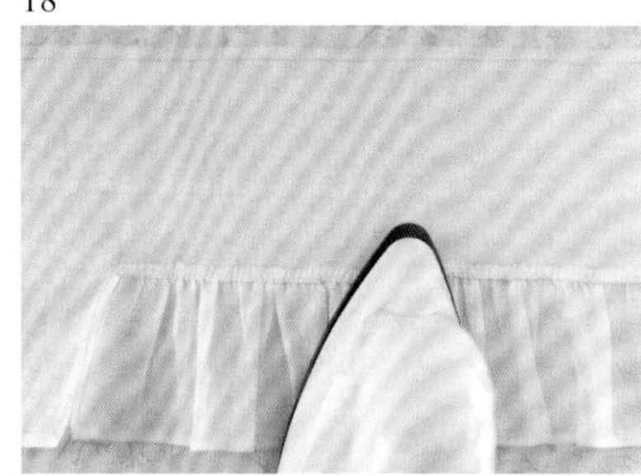

Place the seam allowance up and iron flat.

19

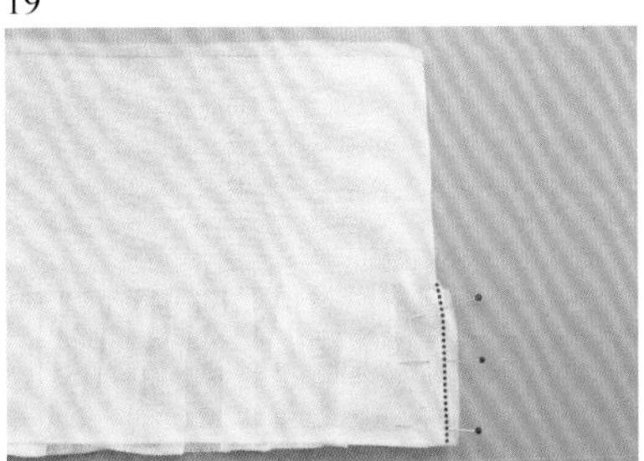

With right sides facing, sew the vertical edges of Skirt A and B together as well. Fold the seam allowance to the B side and iron flat.

20

Place lace of a width of your choosing on the front of the skirt, temporarily fix it with fabric glue, and then sew it.

21

Use a machine to sew two lines of gathering stitches 3 mm (0.12 in) in length in the skirt waist seam allowance.

22

With right sides facing, gather the fabric so the waist width of the bodice aligns with the finished seam in the center of the back of the skirt and sew together.

23

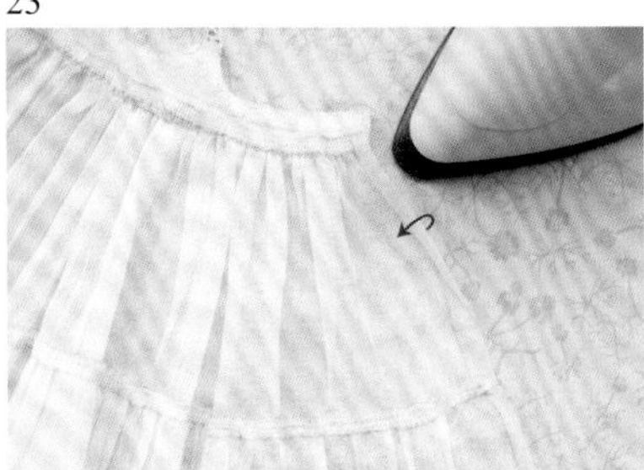

Fold the seam allowance toward the bodice. Then fold the opening at the back of the skirt inwards to slightly below the opening stop marker and iron flat.

24

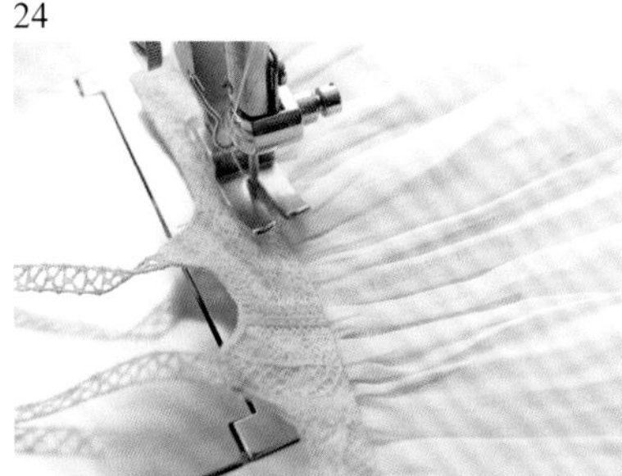

Sew reinforced stitches on the waist bodice section.

25

Sew the diagonally folded back opening.

26

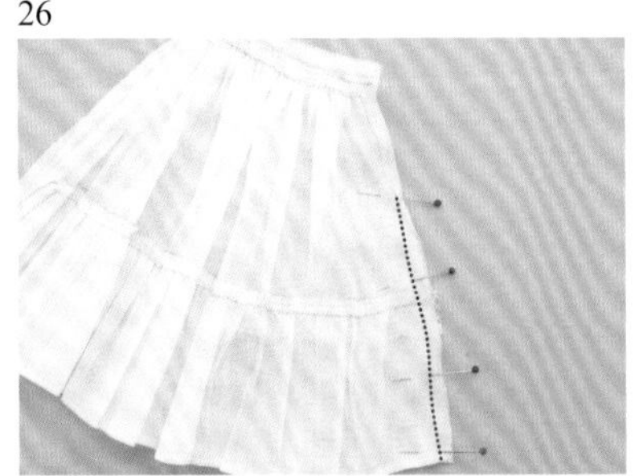

With right sides facing, sew from the skirt hem to the opening stop marker at the center of the back.

27

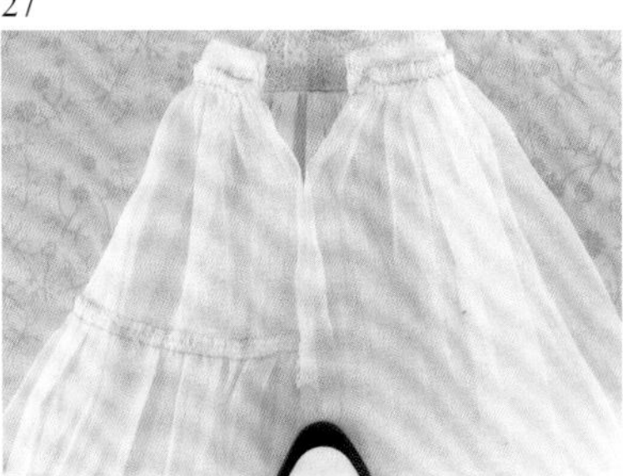

Iron open the seam allowance, turn the piece the right side out and add snaps to complete the dress. Soak the dress in water and allow it to dry naturally to give it a finished look.

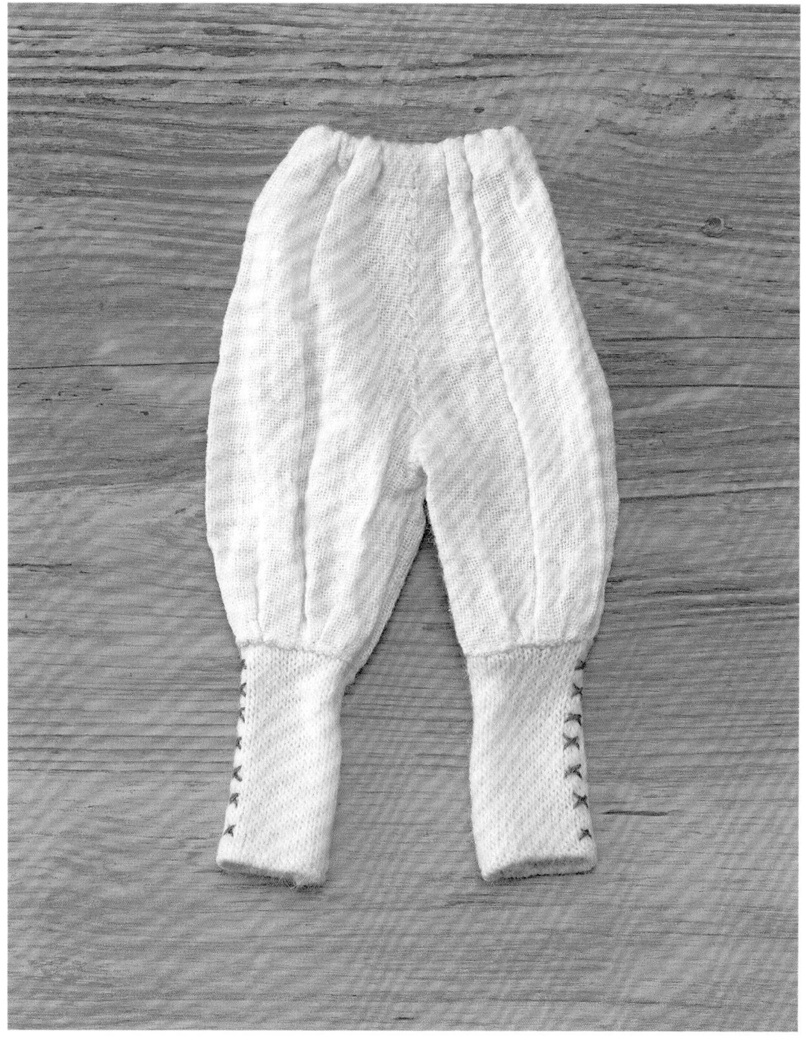

# Sarouel Pants

These pants can be coordinated with many different items.
Make them with dark-colored fabric for a chic look.

| | | | | |
|---|---|---|---|---|
| Cotton linen | S | 24 × 12 cm (9.4 × 4.7 in) | Rib knit | S | 10 × 6 cm (3.9 × 2.4 in) |
| | M | 26 × 15 cm (10.2 × 5.9 in) | | M | 14 × 7 cm (5.5 × 2.8 in) |
| | L | 50 × 25 cm (19.7 × 9.8 in) | | L | 20 × 15 cm (7.9 × 5.9 in) |
| 3 mm (0.12 in) width elastic | | 30 cm (11.8 in) | Cotton embroidery floss | | Ecru, brown |

1

Arrange the paper templates on the fabric and cut out all the sections, then apply fray stopper liquid to all the edges. Use a machine to sew two lines of gathering stitches 2.5 mm (0.1 in) in length in the seam allowance of the pants hem.

2

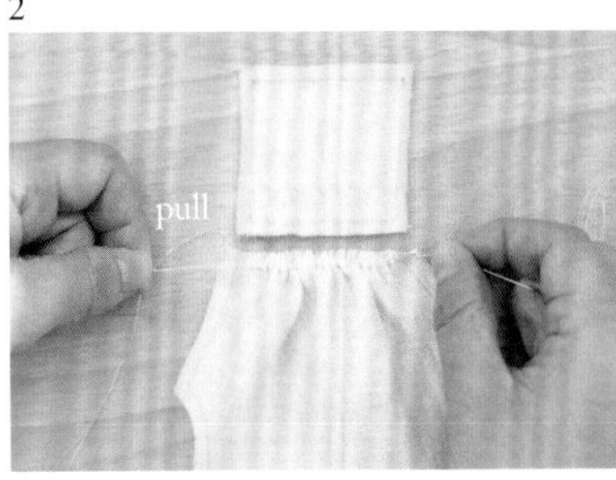


Gather the fabric to match the width of the rib knit (refer to p. 92).

3

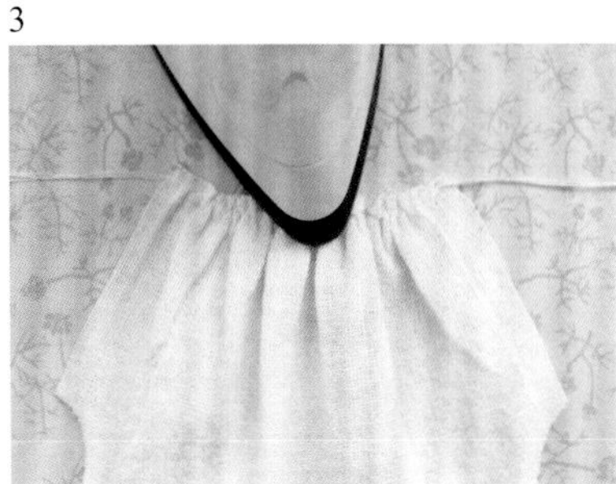

Shape the gathering and iron flat.

4

With right sides facing, sew the pants hem and rib knit together.

5

Place the seam allowance up and iron flat. Fold the seam allowance of the rib hem inwards and iron flat.

6

Sew reinforced stitches on the pants. Sew the rib hem as well.

7

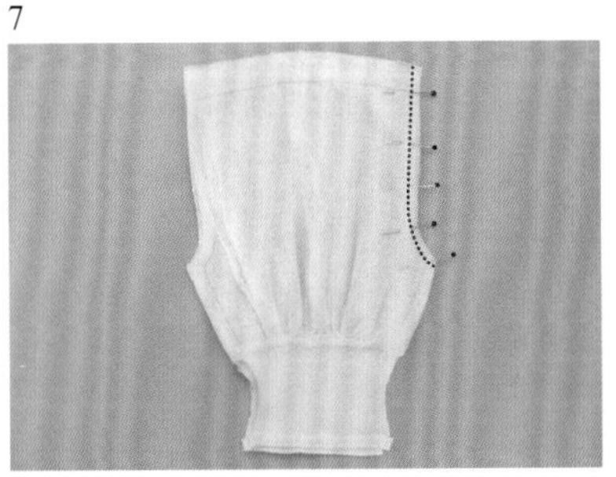

With right sides facing, sew the front pant rise sections together.

8

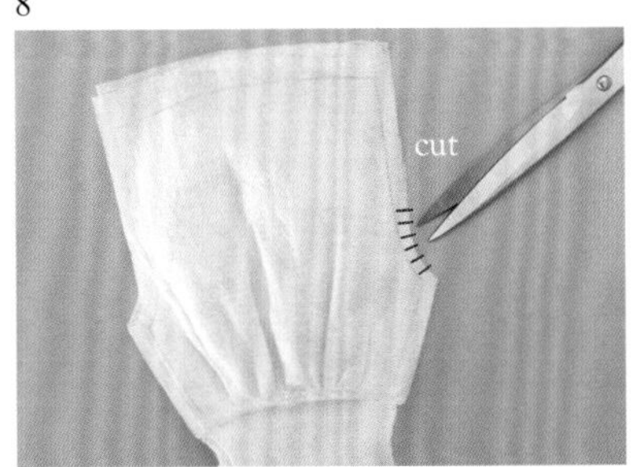


Cut slits in the seam allowance of the front pant rise section. Iron open the seam allowance.

9

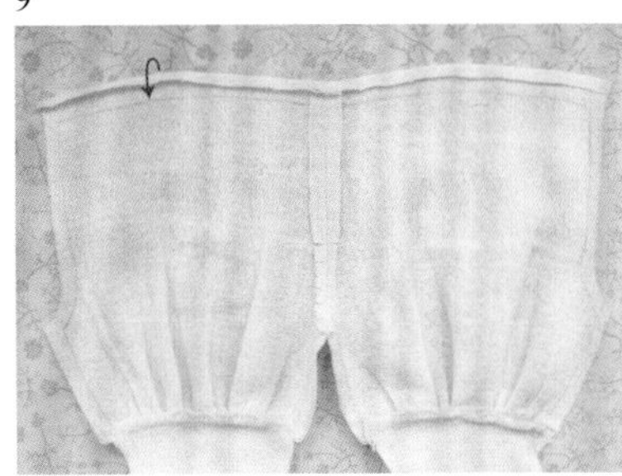

Double-fold the waist seam allowance and iron in place.

10

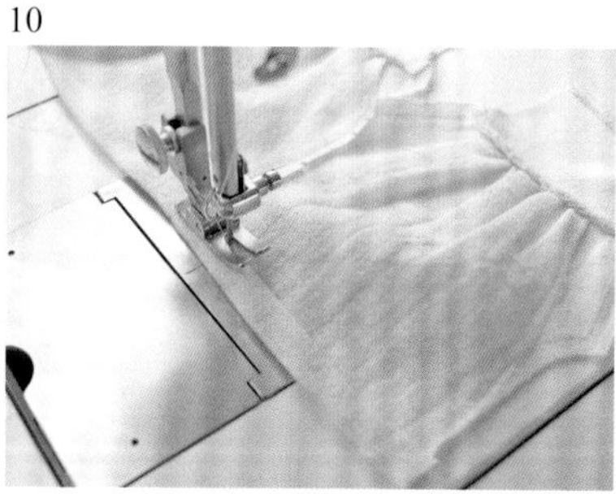

Sew the waist.

11

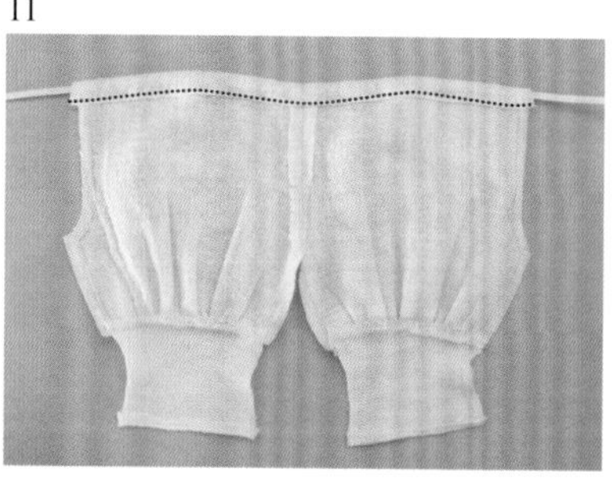

Thread the elastic along the waistband.

12

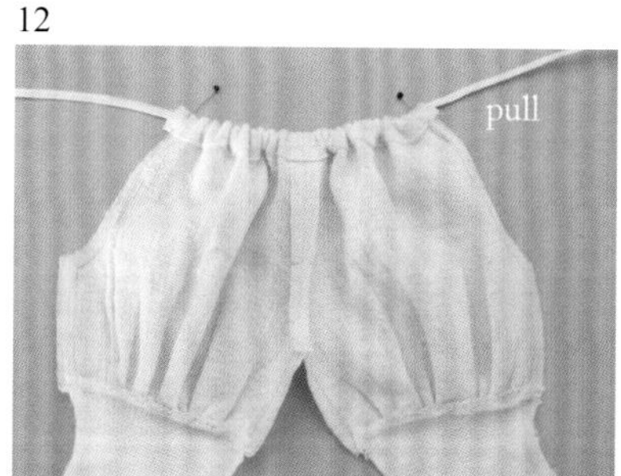


Tighten the waist width to 7.5 cm (3 in) for size S, 9.5 cm (3.7 in) for size M, and 15 cm (5.9 in) for size L and fix with marking pins.

13

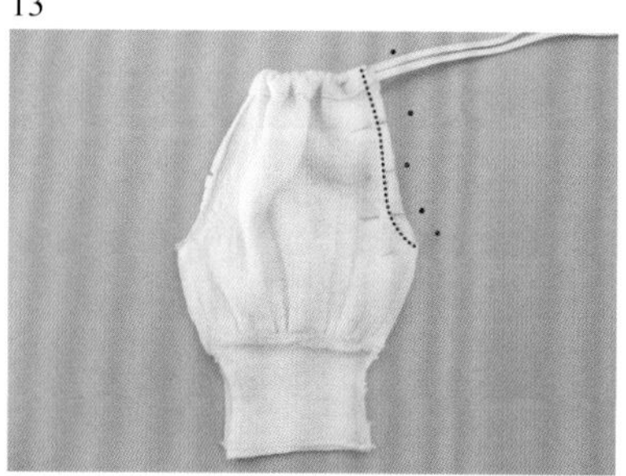

With the right sides facing, align the back pant rise sections and sew together including the elastic.

14

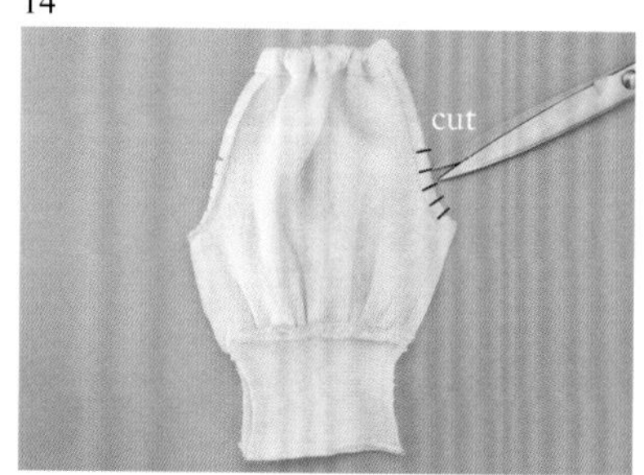


Cut slits in the seam allowance of the back pant rise section. Iron open the seam allowance.

15

With right sides facing, sew the inseams together.

16

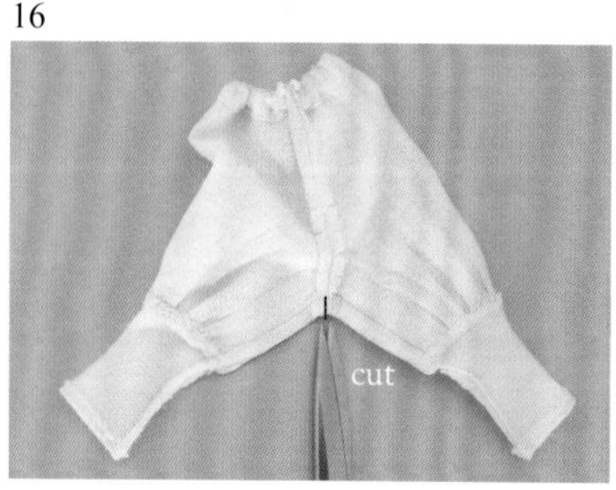


Cut slits into the seam allowance of the inseam.

17

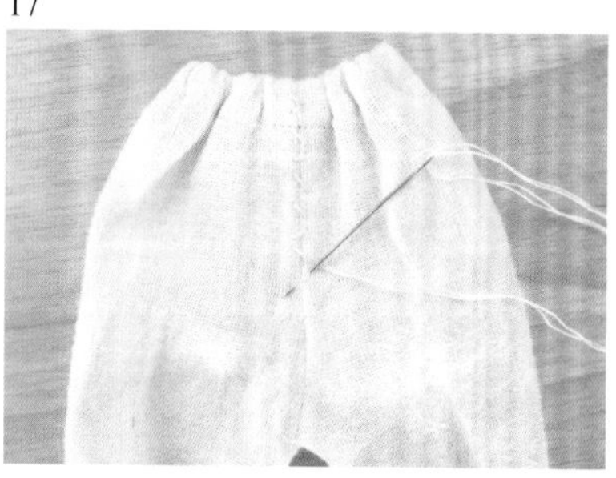

Turn the pants the right side out, iron to shape, and add hand stitches to the pant rise section.

18

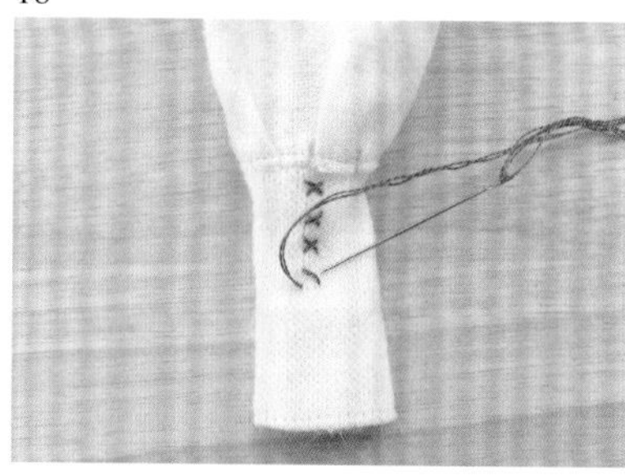

Use brown embroidery floss to make cross stitches on both sides of the rib knit to complete this piece. Soak the pants in water and allow them to dry naturally to give them a finished look.

# Embroidered Smock Dress

A nice dress with extra volume and sleeves that are easy to attach.
Enjoy adding your favorite embroidery or try changing the length to make a lovely blouse.

| | | | |
|---|---|---|---|
| Linen | S 30 × 30 cm (11.8 × 11.8 in)<br>M 42 × 32 cm (16.5 × 12.6 in)<br>L 90 × 55 cm (35.4 × 21.7 in) | Cotton bias | S 2 cm width × 11 cm (0.8 × 4.3 in)<br>M 3 cm width × 12 cm (1.2 × 4.7 in)<br>L 3 cm width × 20 cm (1.2 × 7.9 in) |
| Snaps | S, M 1 pair L 2 pairs | Cotton embroidery floss | Navy blue or deep red |

1

Trace the sleeve template on to the linen fabric, cut widely around it, and set in an embroidery hoop.

2

Take a single strand of embroidery floss. First, sew two lines of back stitch along the center (for size L, do chain stitch).

3

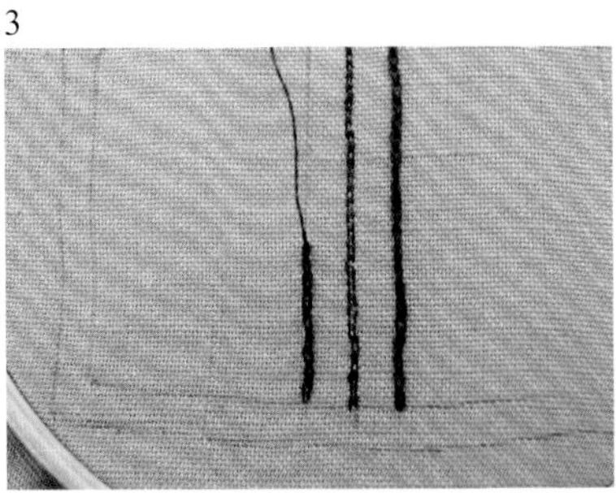

Sew small chain stitches on the left and right.

4

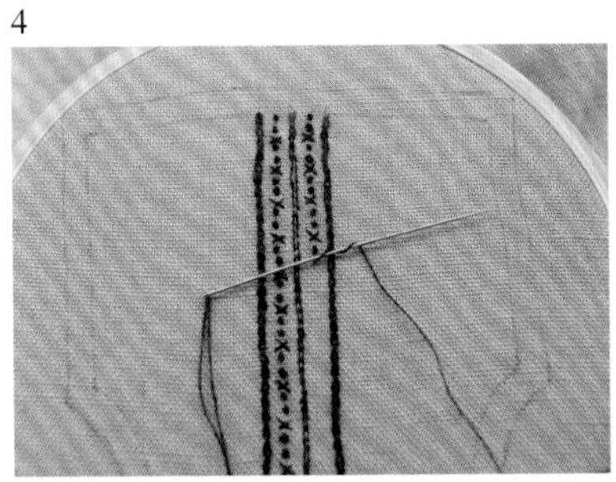

Sew French knots and cross stitches between the three lines.

5

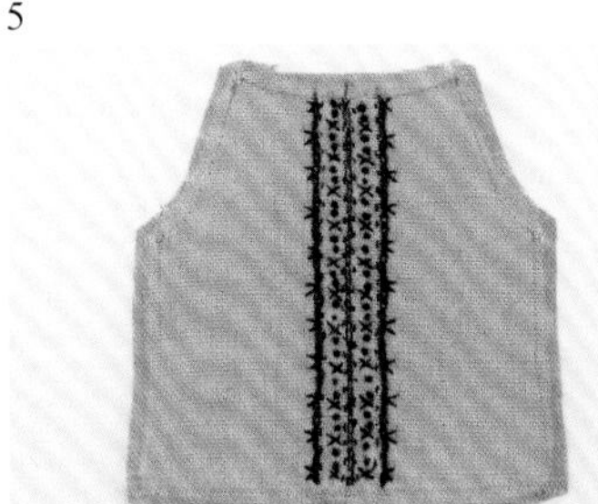

Sew running stitches along the center line and in the lines to the left and right. Then add V-shaped stitches to both edges. When the embroidery is completed, cut the sleeves to size and apply fray stopper liquid to the edges.

6

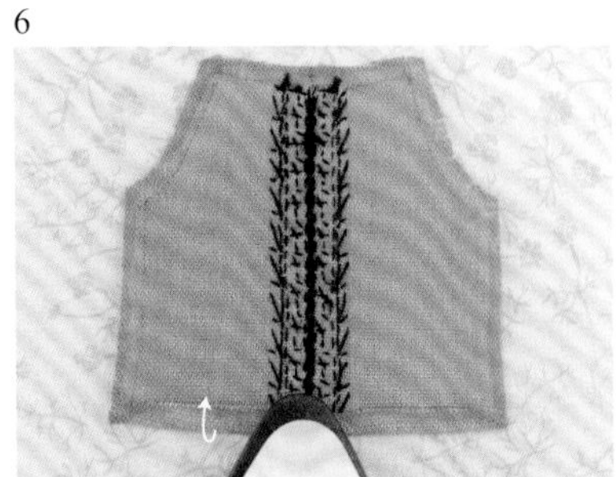

Fold the seam allowance of the sleeve opening inwards and iron flat.

7

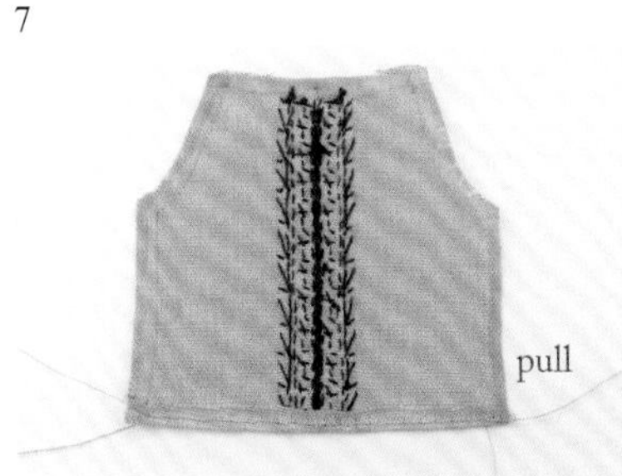


Use a machine to sew one line of gathering stitches 3 mm (0.12 in) in length in the seam allowance of the sleeve opening. Then pull the threads to gather the fabric (refer to p. 92).

8

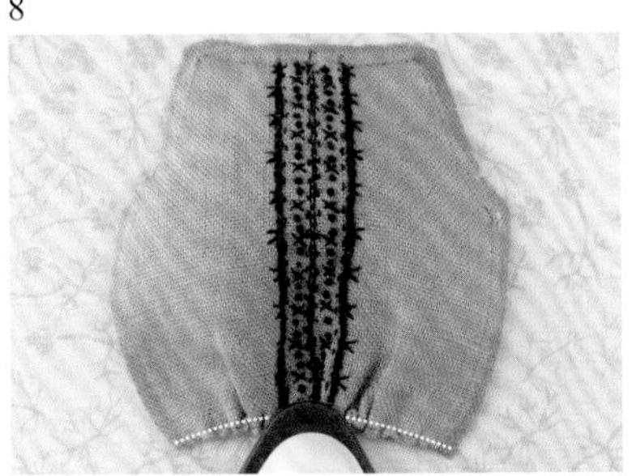

Gather the fabric so that it measures 4 cm (1.6 in) for size S, 5 cm (2 in) for size M, and 7.5 cm (3 in) for size L (not including the seam allowance) and tie the threads. Then iron in place and sew reinforced stitches.

9

With right sides facing, sew the front bodice section and the sleeves together.

10

Continue by sewing the back bodice section and the sleeves together with right sides facing.

11

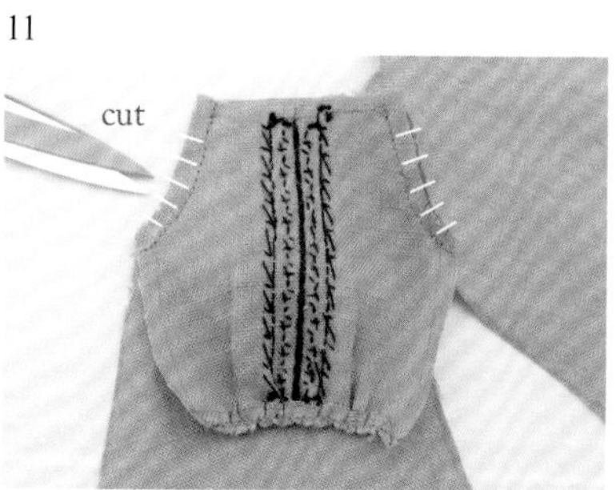


Cut slits 5 mm (0.2 in) apart in the seam allowances of the bodice and sleeves.

12

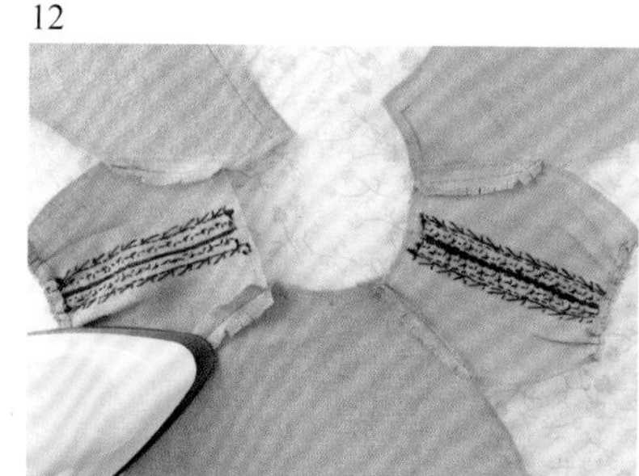

Iron open the seam allowances.

13

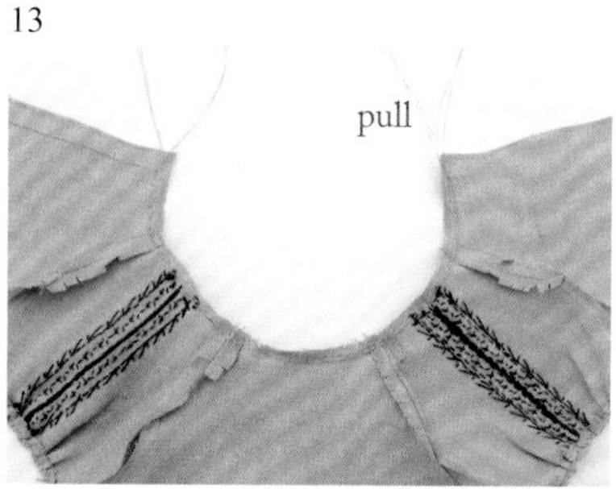


Use a machine to sew two lines of gathering stitches 3 mm (0.12 in) in length in the neckline seam allowance.

14

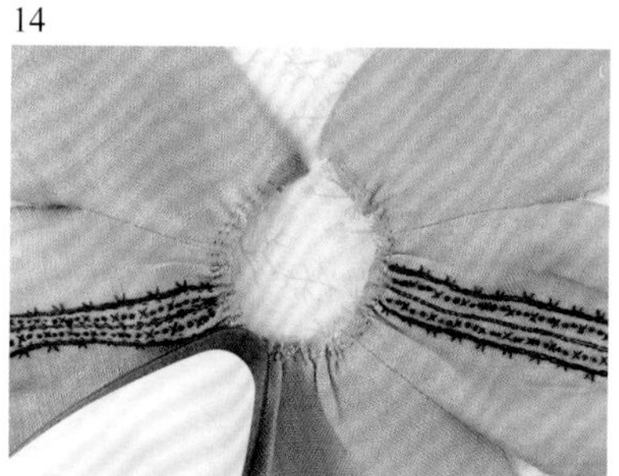

Gather the fabric to the width of the neckline bias* and iron to shape. (*Cut on a 45-degree angle or use bias tape.)

15

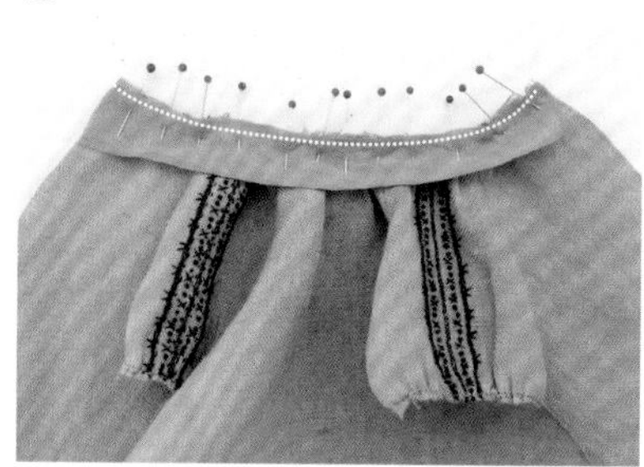

With right sides facing, sew the bodice neckline and neckline bias together.

16

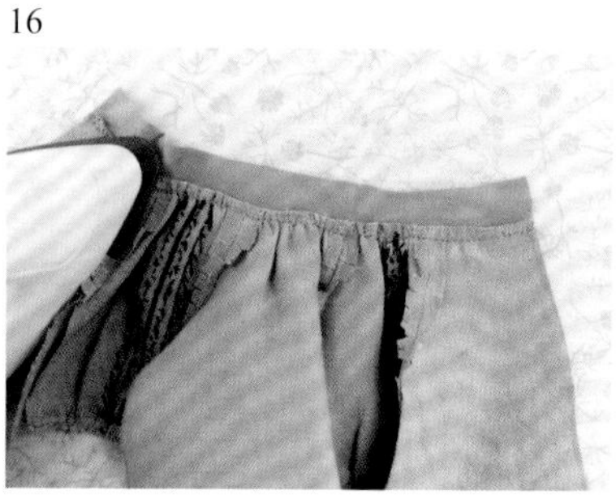

Place the seam allowance up and iron flat.

17

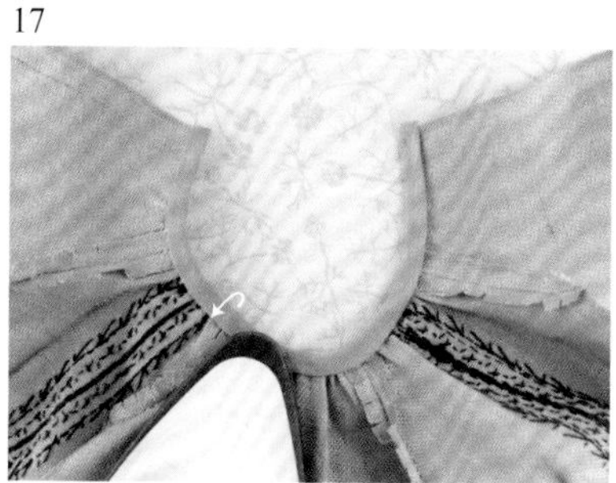

Use an iron to double-fold the bias so it wraps around the neckline seam allowance.

18

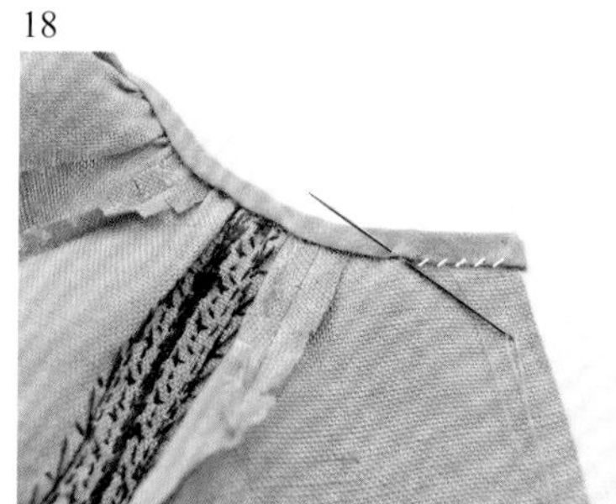

Sew the bias hem with blind stitches to close up the neckline.

19

The completed neckline.

20

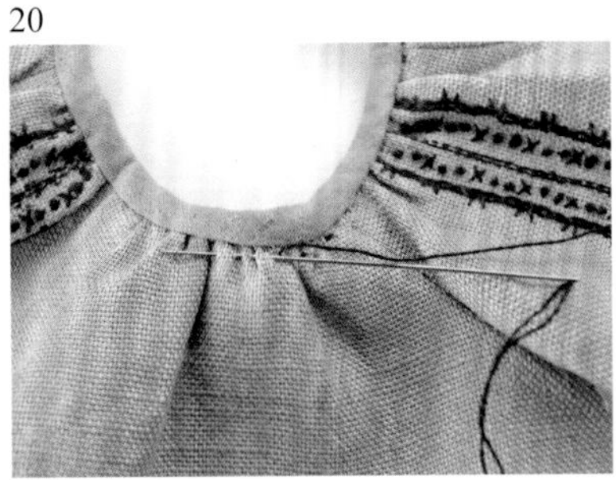

Use one strand of embroidery floss to sew running stitches along the front of the bodice neckline.

21

With the right sides of the front and back bodice sections facing, sew them together from the sleeve openings along under the arms and down to the hem.

22

Cut slits under the arms. Turn the piece right side out and iron open the seam allowance.

23

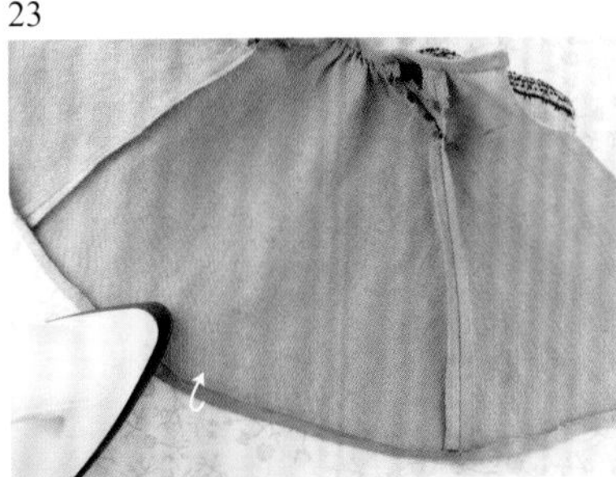

Fold the seam allowance of the bodice hem inwards and iron flat.

24

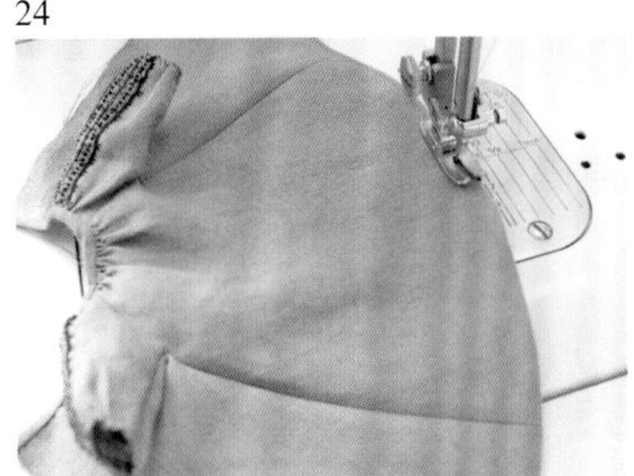

Sew the hem.

25

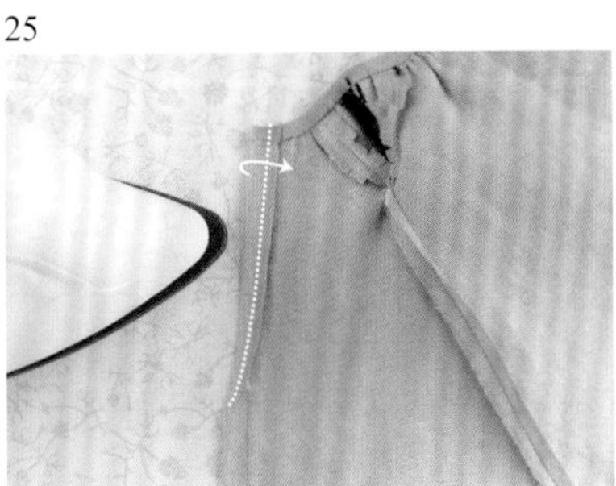

Fold the back opening inwards slightly below the opening stop marker, iron flat and sew it.

26

With right sides facing, sew from the hem to the opening stop marker at the center of the back. Iron open the seam allowances.

27

Turn the piece the right side out and add snaps to complete the dress. Soak the dress in water, then gently wring it and allow to dry to give it a natural look.

# Waist Apron

Linen is great for creating a well-worn look.
This may be a simple piece, but it is the perfect addition to any natural style wardrobe.

| | | |
|---|---|---|
| Linen | S | 42 × 10 cm (16.5 × 3.9 in) |
| | M | 44 × 14 cm (17.3 × 5.5 in) |
| | L | 73 × 25 cm (28.7 × 9.8 in) |

1

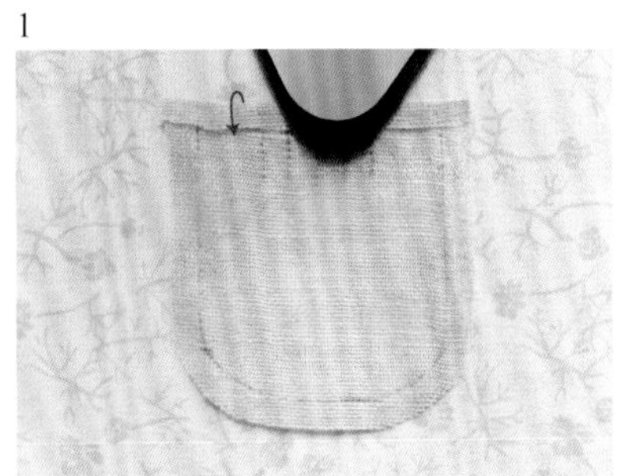

Arrange the paper templates on the fabric and cut out all the sections, then apply fray stopper liquid to the edges. Fold the seam allowance of the top of the pocket and iron flat.

2

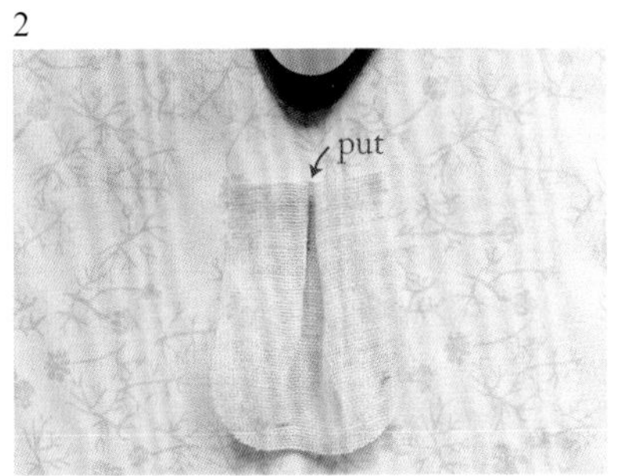


Fold the tucks and temporarily fix them with fabric glue.

3

Sew the top of the pocket.

4

Sew running stitches 3 mm (0.12 in) in length on the curved sections of the pocket.

5

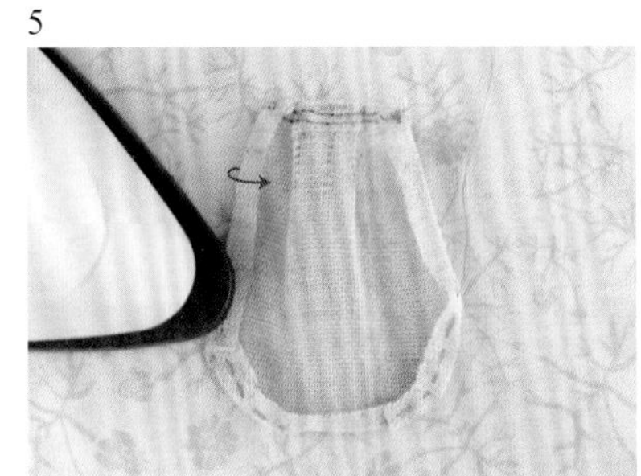

Pull the running stitches to gather the fabric and form curves, then iron to shape.

6

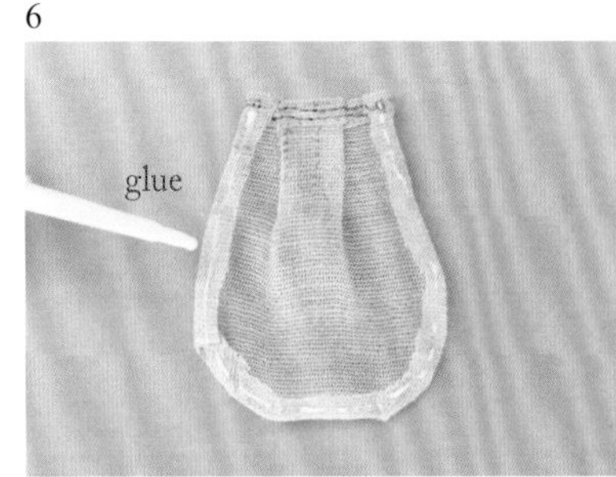


Apply fabric glue to the seam allowance and temporarily fix the pocket in place on the apron.

7

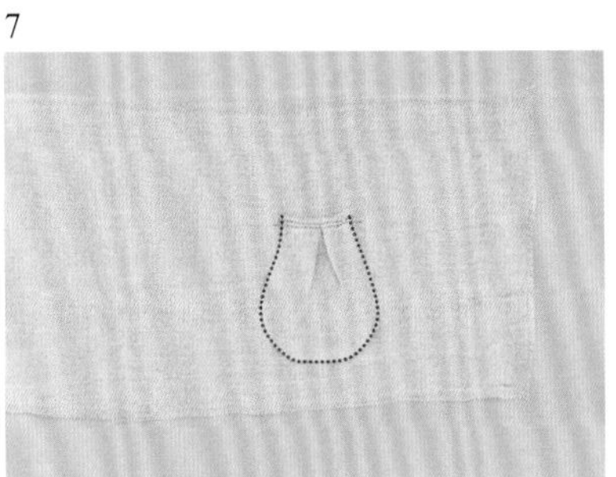

Sew the pocket in place.

8

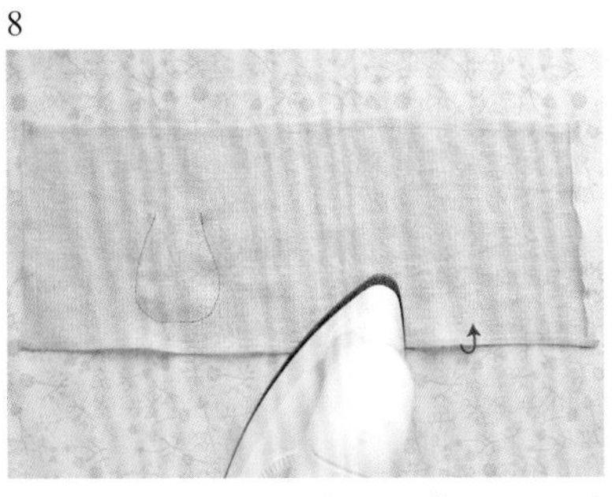

Fold the apron hem and seam allowances of both sides inwards and iron flat.

9

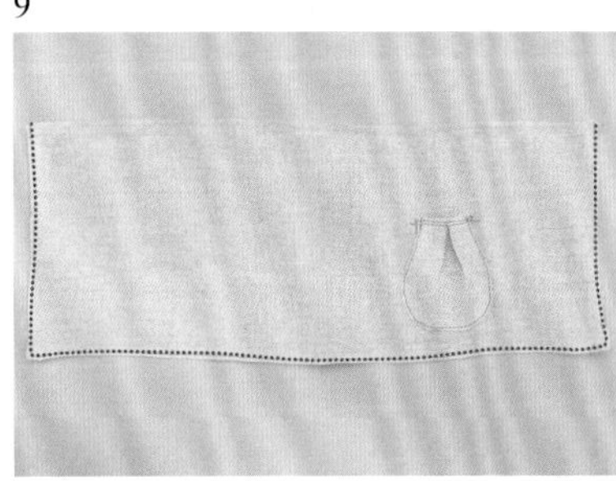

Sew the sides and hem.

10

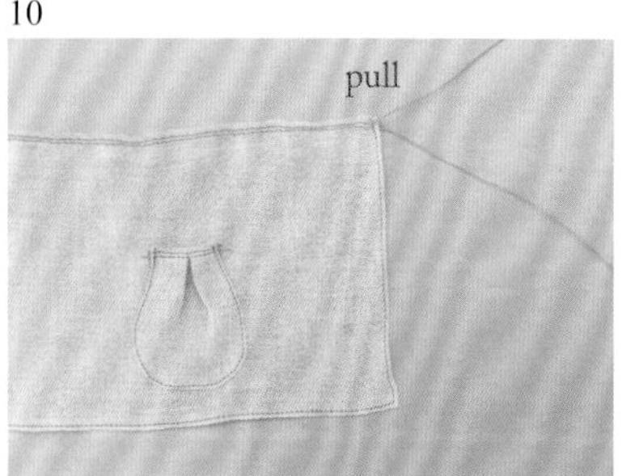


Use a machine to sew two lines of gathering stitches 3 mm (0.12 in) in length in the seam allowance of the apron waist (refer to p. 92).

11

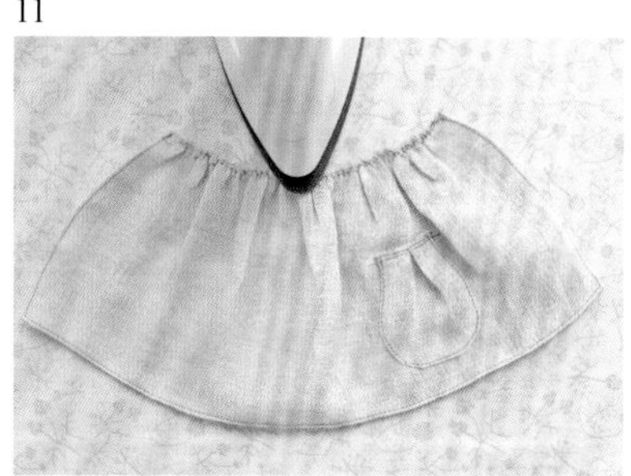

Gather the fabric so that it measures 7 cm (2.8 in) for size S, 10 cm (3.9 in) for size M, and 14.5 cm (5.7 in) for size L, then iron in place.

12

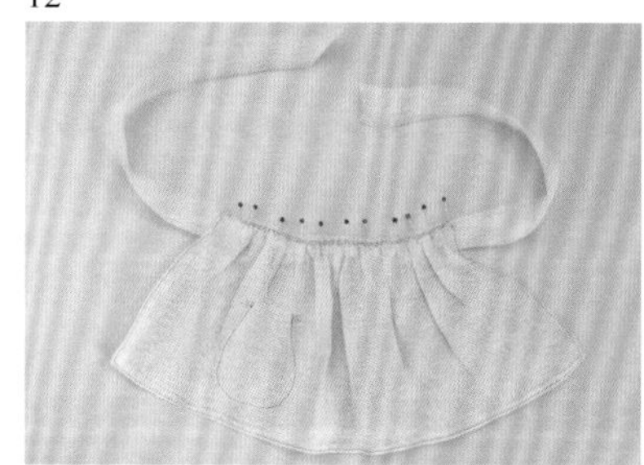

Place the apron and waist cord with right sides facing and fix from the center with marking pins.

13

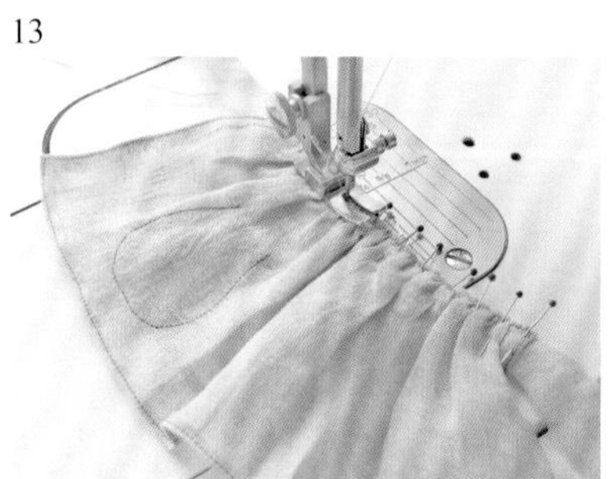

Sew the waist cord on to the apron.

14

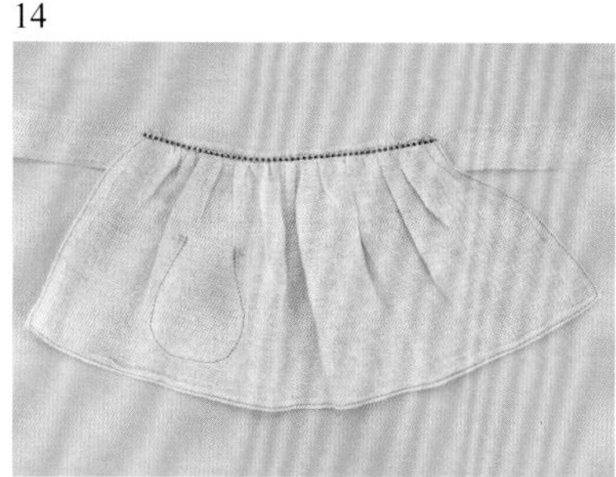

Place the seam allowance up.

15

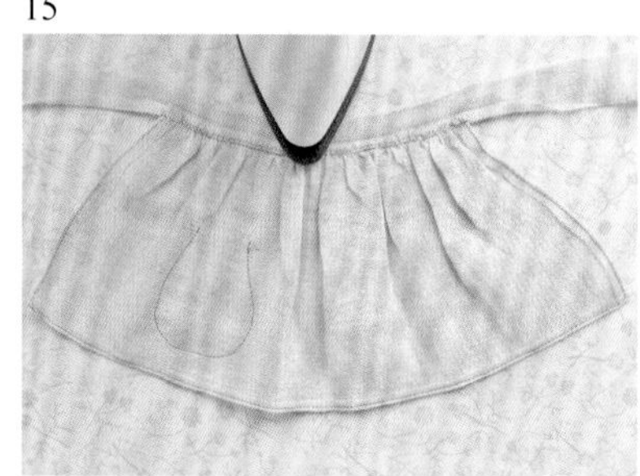

Fold back the waist cord and iron flat.

16

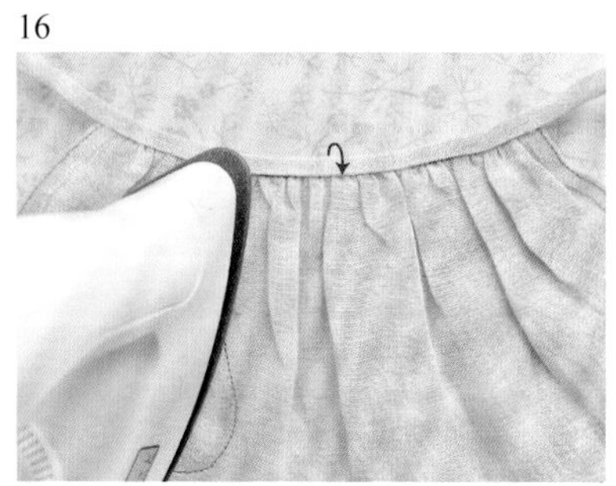

Double-fold the waist cord so it wraps around the seam allowance and iron to shape.

17

Sew reinforced stitches along the waist cord.

18

Soak the apron in water, then gently wring it and allow to dry to give it a natural look.

# Peter Pan Collar Dress

Enjoy choosing matching colors for the small collar, bib, and cuffs.
For ease, try making the detailed pin tucks broader or swap for a piece of lovely intricate lace.

| Material | Size | Amount |
|---|---|---|
| Patterned cotton lawn | S | 30 × 20 cm (11.8 × 7.9 in) |
| | M | 50 × 20 cm (19.7 × 7.9 in) |
| | L | 105 × 25 cm (41.3 × 9.8 in) |
| Plain cotton lawn | S | 20 × 10 cm (7.9 × 3.9 in) |
| | M | 30 × 10 cm (11.8 × 3.9 in) |
| | L | 40 × 15 cm (15.7 × 5.9 in) |

| Material | Size | Amount |
|---|---|---|
| 4 mm (0.16 in) lace | S | 14 cm (5.5 in) |
| | M | 19 cm (7.5 in) |
| | L | 35 cm (13.8 in) |
| Snaps | S, M | 2 pairs |
| | L | 3 pairs |
| Cotton embroidery floss | | Coral |

1

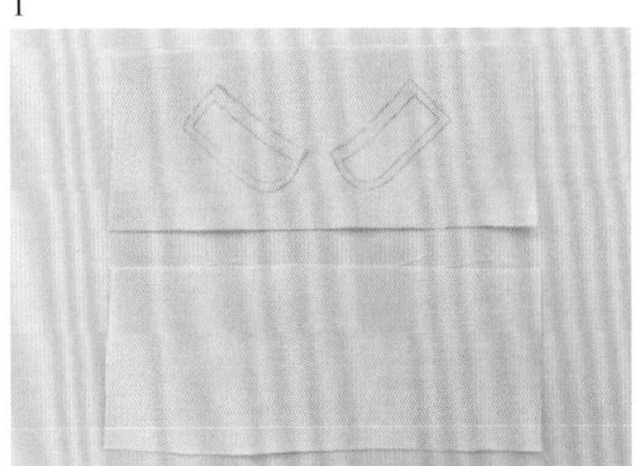

Trace a pair of collars on to the fabric and cut widely around them. Prepare another piece of fabric the same size.

2

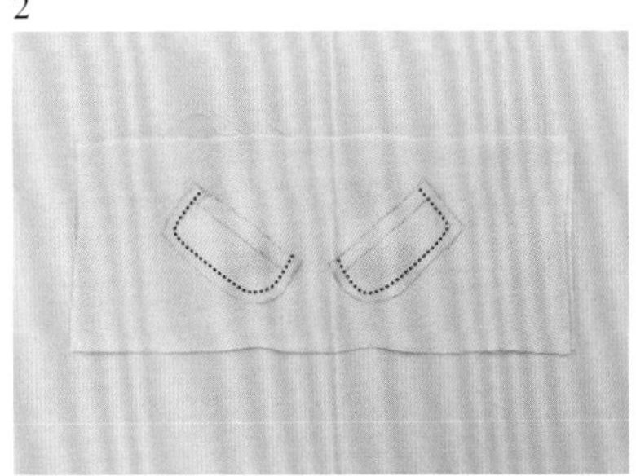

Place on the second piece of fabric with right sides facing and sew along the outer seam line.

3

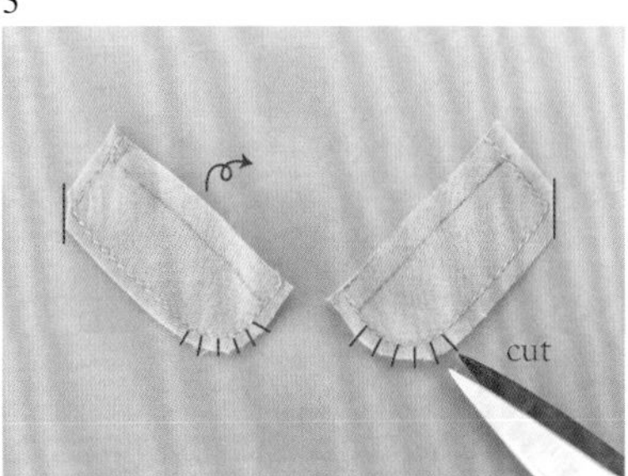


Cut the collar sections out, leaving the seam allowances. Fold the corners of the seam allowances, cutting fine slits where the fabric curves. Be careful not to cut the stitches.

4

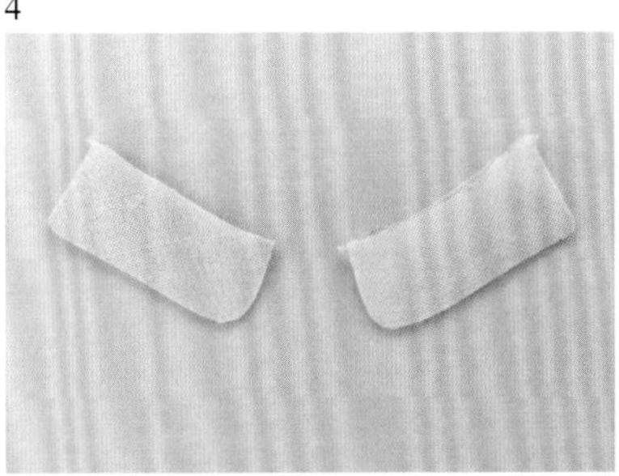

Turn the piece the right side out, using a tailor's awl or tweezers to neatly push out the corners and curves, then iron to shape.

5

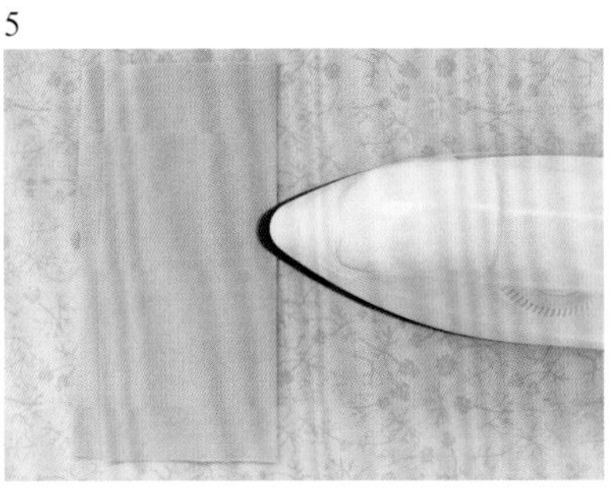

Make the pin tucks on the bib. Fold a piece of fabric cut larger than the bib template along the weave and iron.

6

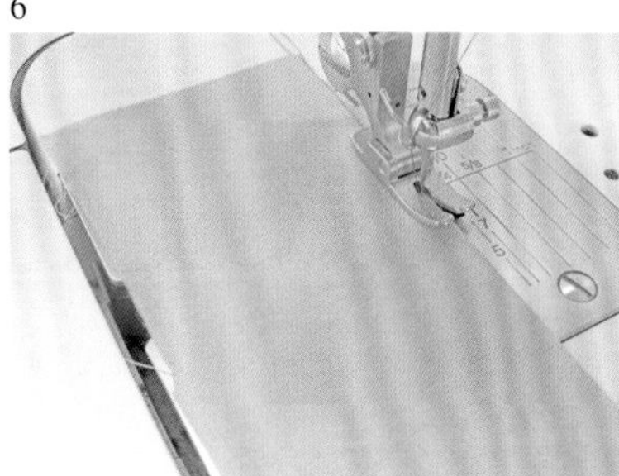

Machine sew a straight line 1 mm (0.04 in) from the fold.

7

The first fold neatly sewn.

8

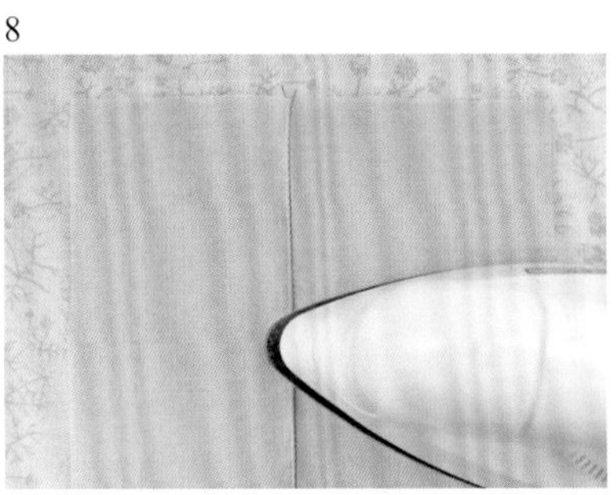

Open the fabric out and iron the 1 mm (0.04 in) sewn fold so that it faces out.

9

Next make a pin tuck on the other side. Fold the cloth again using an iron 6 mm (0.24 in) from the first fold.

10

Machine sew a straight line 1 mm (0.04 in) from the fold.

11

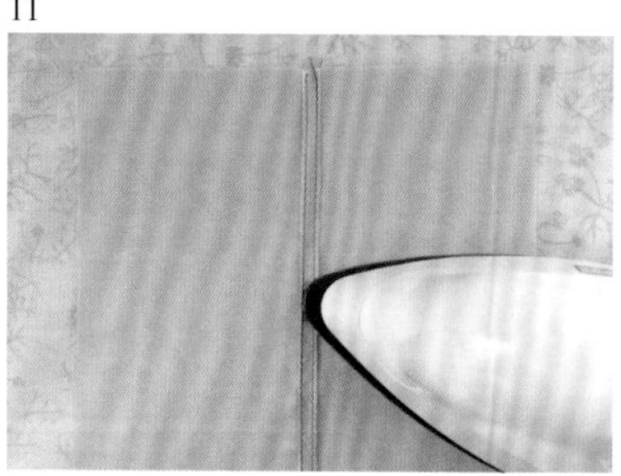

Open the fabric out and turn the fold over to the other side, then iron to shape.

12

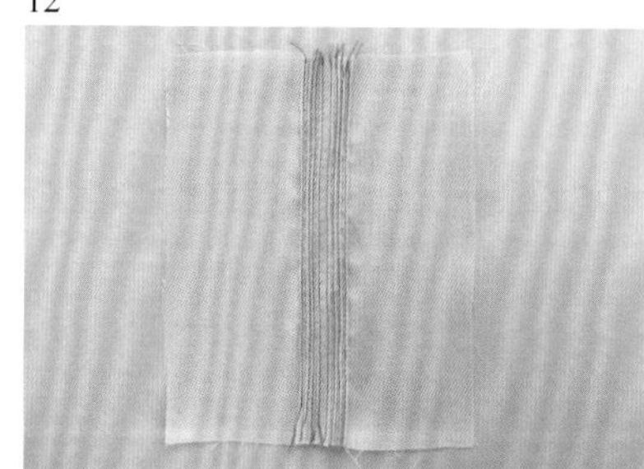

Fold the fabric 3 mm (0.12 in) from the last fold and iron, then sew 1 mm (0.04 in) from that new fold and turn the fold to face outwards. Repeat this step to create the pin tucks.

13

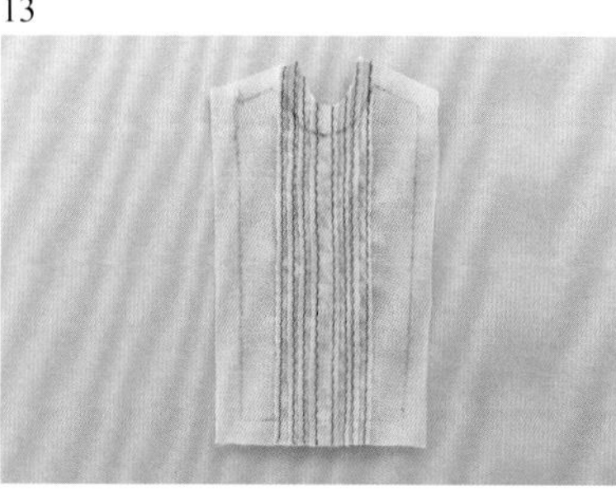

Trace the bib template on the fabric with the pin tucks in the center and cut the section. Cut out the other sections and apply fray stopper liquid to the edges.

14

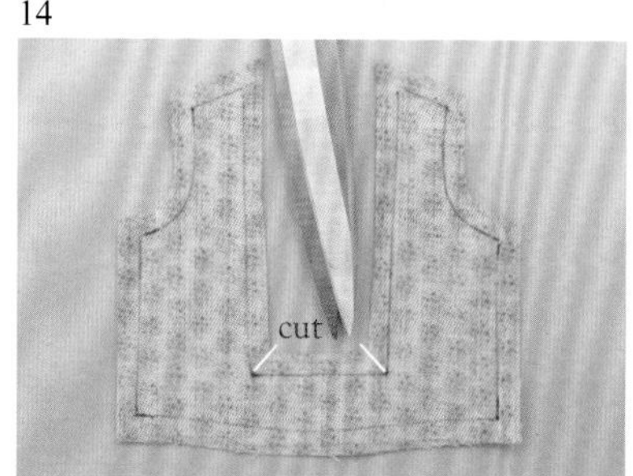


Cut slits into the corners of the front bodice seam allowance.

15

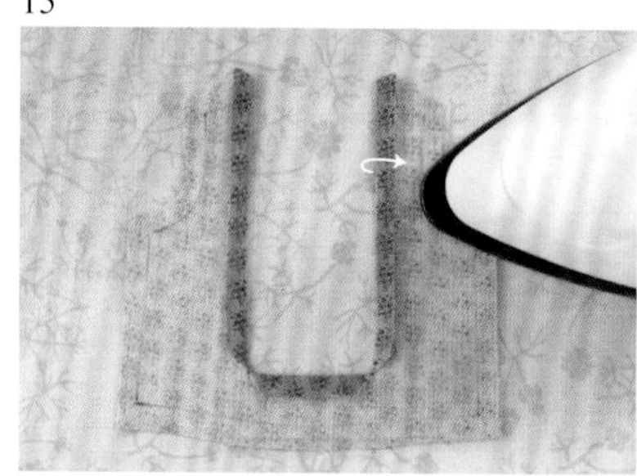

Fold the seam allowance inwards and iron flat.

16

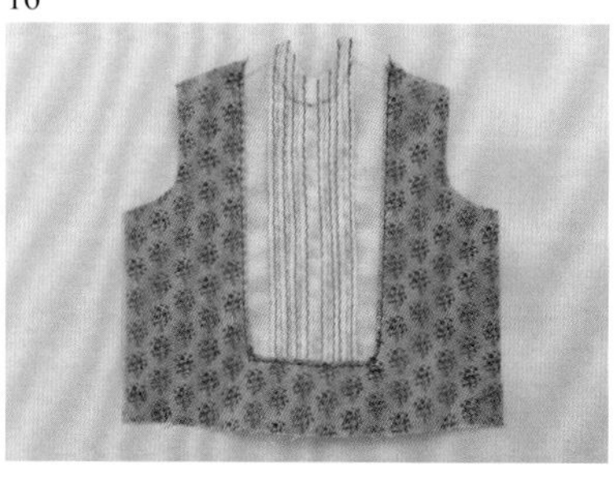

Temporarily fix the bib on the front bodice with fabric glue and machine sew together.

17

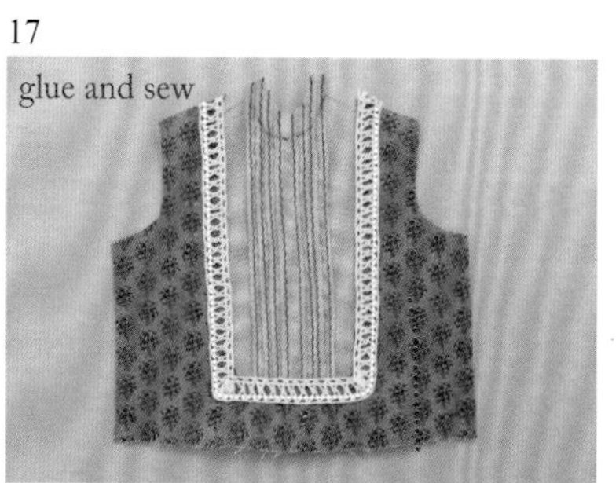


Place lace along the edge of the bib, temporarily fix it with fabric glue, and then sew it.

18

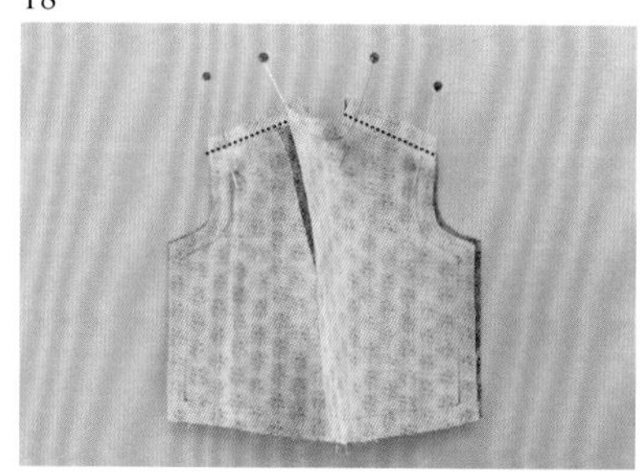

With the right sides of the front and back bodice sections facing, sew the shoulders.

19

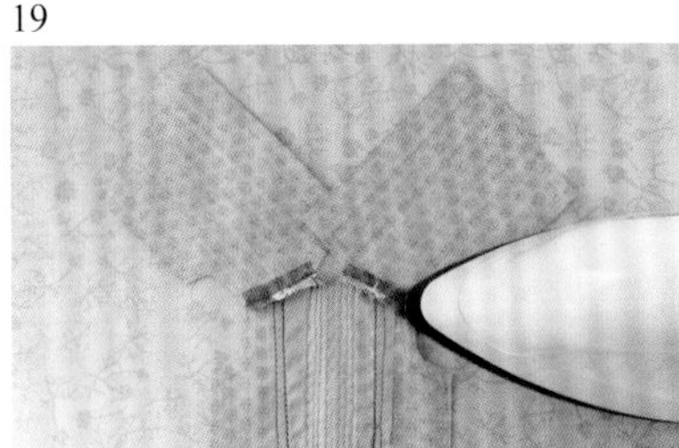

Iron open the seam allowances.

20

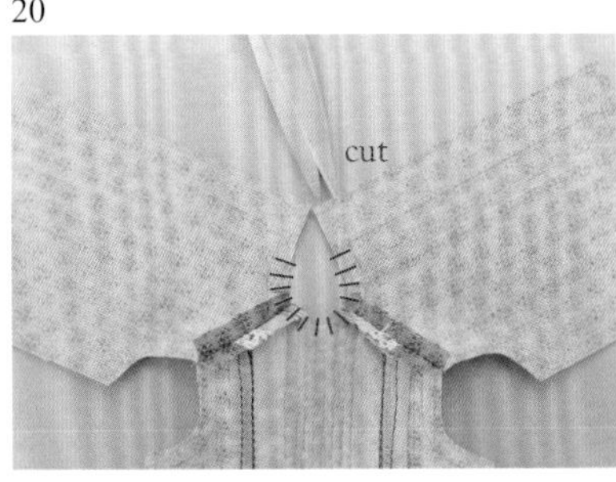


Cut fine slits into the seam allowance of the neckline.

21

Apply fabric glue to the seam allowance.

22

Temporarily fix the collar so that it is even on both sides of the bib center and sew in place.

23

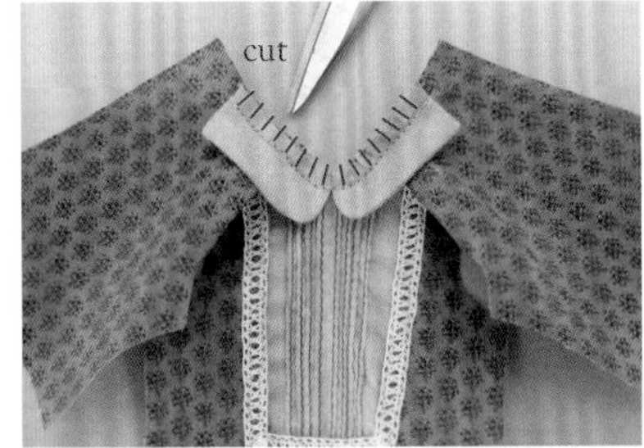


Cut fine slits into the seam allowance of the collar.

24

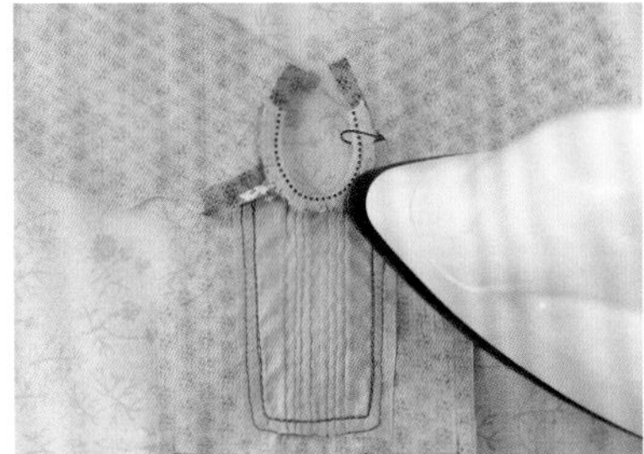

Fold the seam allowance of the collar to the back, iron to shape, and sew reinforced stitches on the neckline.

25

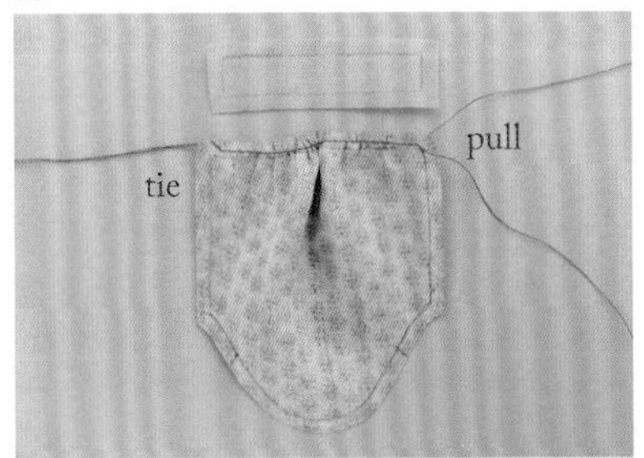


Machine sew one line of gathering stitches 2.5 mm (0.1 in) in length in the seam allowance of the sleeve opening. Then gather the fabric to match the width of the cuffs (refer to p. 92).

26

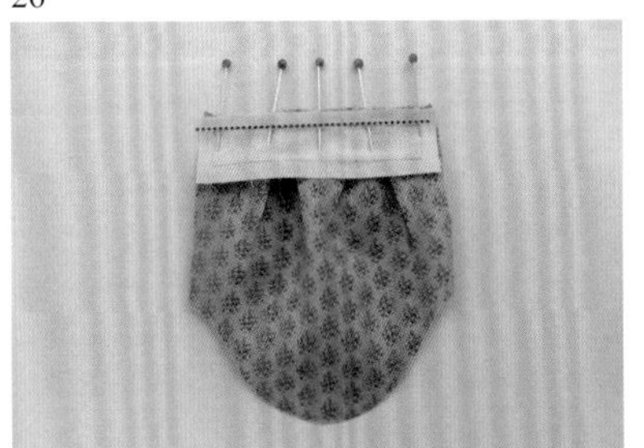

Iron the gathering to shape, then with right sides facing, sew the cuffs and sleeve openings together.

27

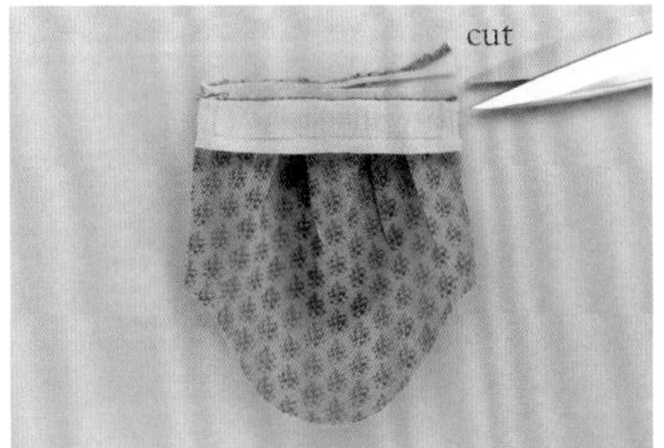


Cut the seam allowance of the sleeve and cuff to 3 mm (0.12 in) in width.

28

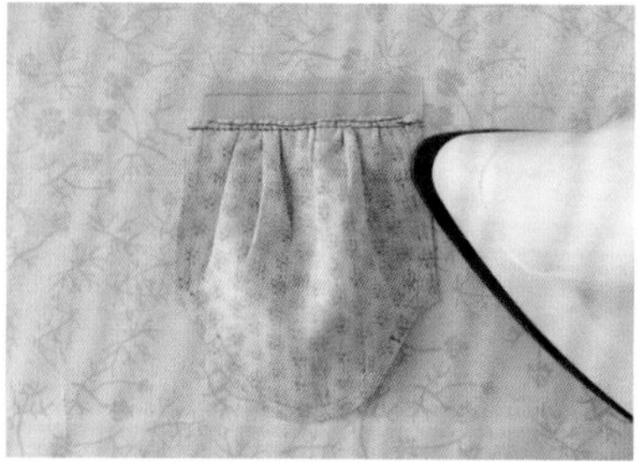

Use an iron to double-fold the cuffs so they wrap around the seam allowance.

29

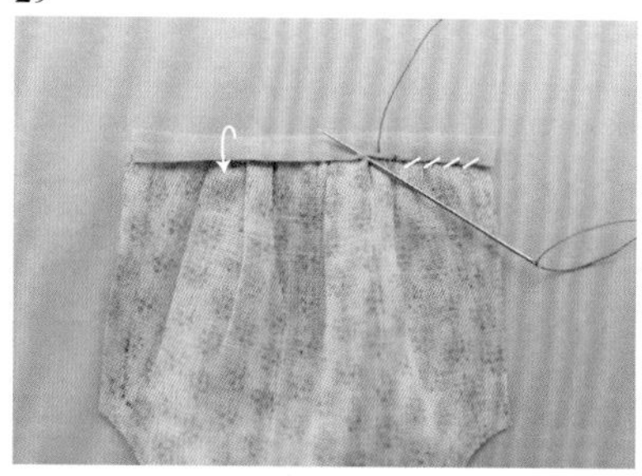

Sew the cuff hems with blind stitches to close them up.

30

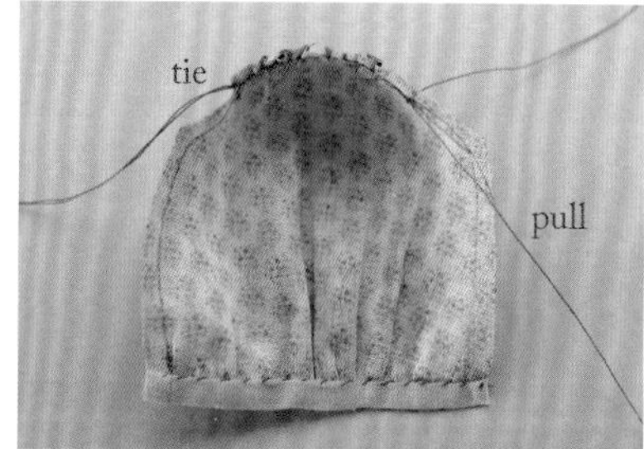


Machine sew one line of gathering stitches 2.5 mm (0.1 in) in length in the sleeve cap seam allowances from marker to marker. Gather the fabric to match the width of the bodice armholes.

31

With right sides facing, sew the bodice section and the sleeves together. Raise the machine presser foot a number of times while sewing to gradually align the seam allowances of the sleeve caps and armholes.

32

The sleeves are now attached to the bodice. Place the seam allowance toward the sleeves and iron flat.

33

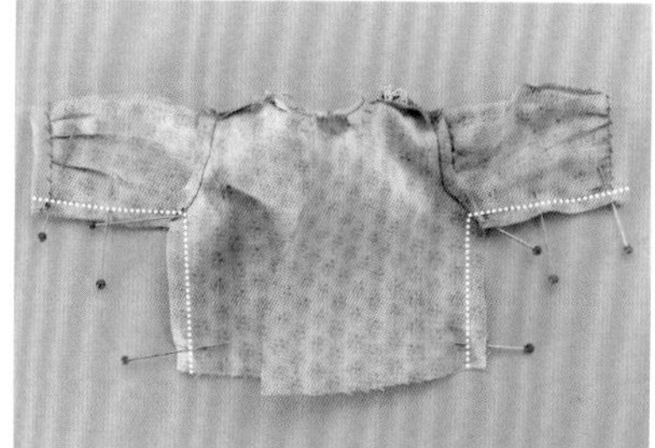

With the right sides of the front and back bodice sections facing, sew them together from the sleeve openings along under the arms and down to the hem.

34

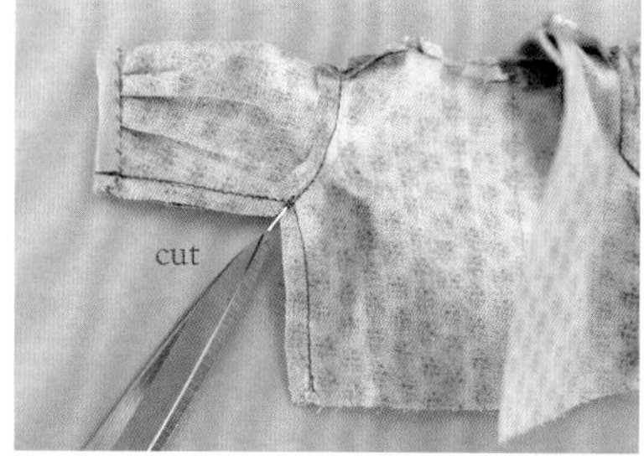


Cut slits into the seam allowance under the arms. Turn the piece right side out and iron open the seam allowance.

35

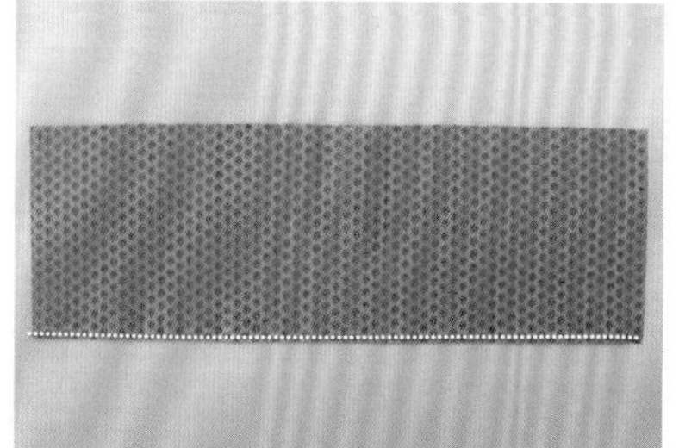

Fold the seam allowance of the skirt hem inwards with an iron and sew.

36

Machine sew two lines of gathering stitches 2.5 mm (0.1 in) in length in the waist seam allowance. Gather the fabric to match the width of the bodice waist (refer to p. 92).

37

With right sides facing, sew the bodice and the skirt waist together.

38

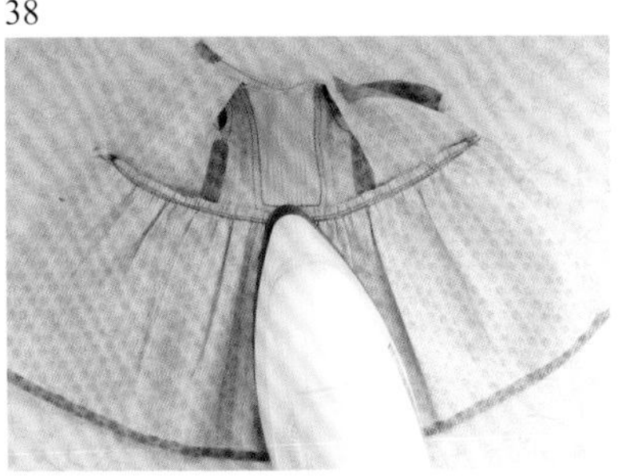

Fold the seam allowance to the bodice section and iron flat.

39

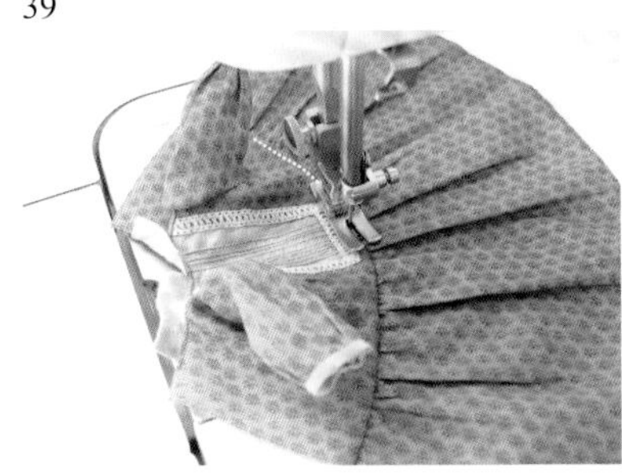

Sew reinforced stitches on the waist bodice section.

40

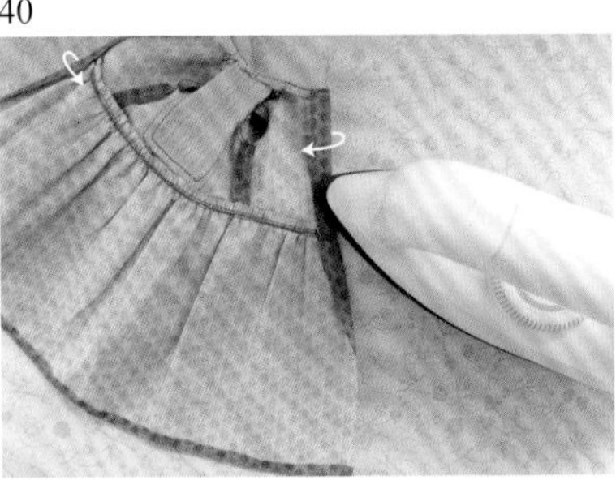

Fold the back opening inwards slightly below the opening stop marker and iron flat.

41

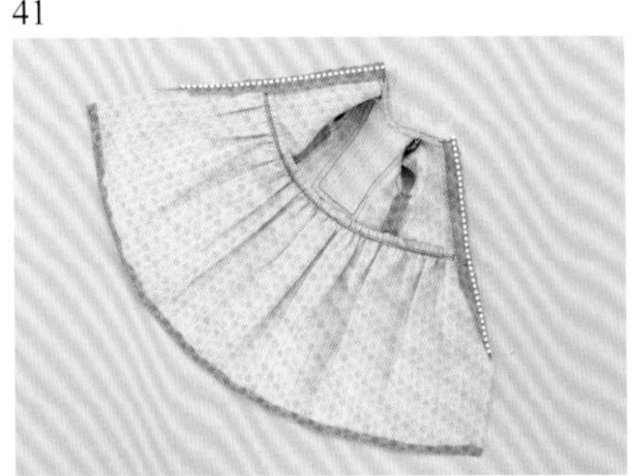

Sew the back opening.

42

With right sides facing, sew from the hem to the opening stop marker at the center of the back.

43

Iron open the seam allowance and turn the piece the right side out.

44

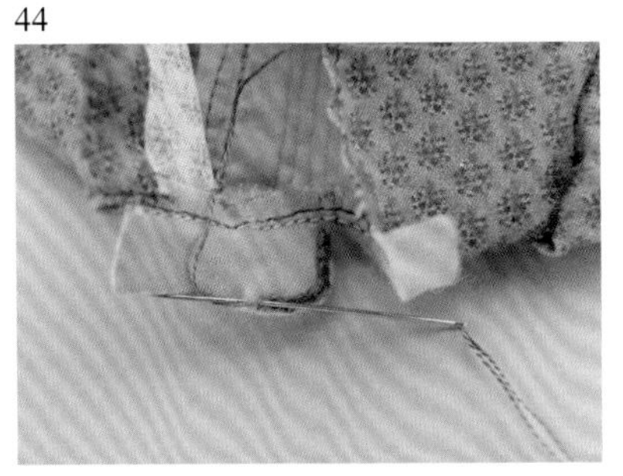

Use one strand of embroidery floss to sew chain stitches along the edge of the collar.

45

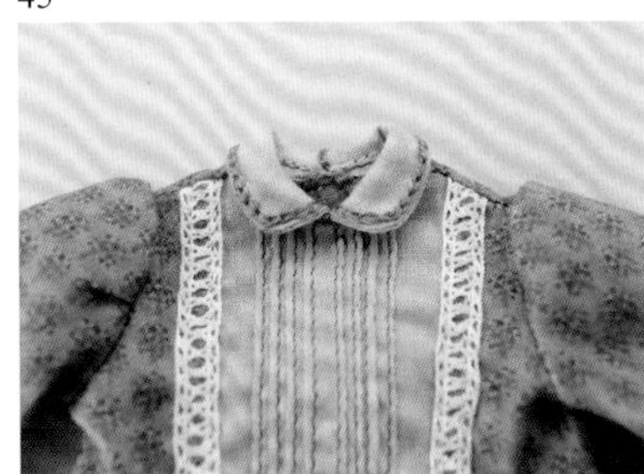

Add snaps to the back opening to complete the dress.

# Blouse

The darts on this blouse create a lovely silhouette.
For a more everyday look, try omitting the lace.

| | | | | | |
|---|---|---|---|---|---|
| Striped cotton lawn | S | 20 × 17 cm (7.9 × 6.7 in) | 8 mm (0.31 in) lace | S | collar 12 cm (4.7 in), sleeves 6 cm (2.4 in) × 2 |
| | M | 25 × 20 cm (9.8 × 7.9 in) | | M | collar 16 cm (6.3 in), sleeves 8 cm (3.1 in) × 2 |
| | L | 55 × 20 cm (21.7 × 7.9 in) | | L | collar 24 cm (9.4 in), sleeves 12 cm (4.7 in) × 2 |
| Plain cotton lawn | S | 12 × 6 cm (4.7 × 2.4 in) | 2.5 mm (0.1 in) buttons | S, M | 2 pieces L 6 pieces |
| | M | 15 × 10 cm (5.9 × 3.9 in) | | | |
| | L | 20 × 15 cm (7.9 × 5.9 in) | Snaps | S, M | 2 pairs L 5 pairs |

1

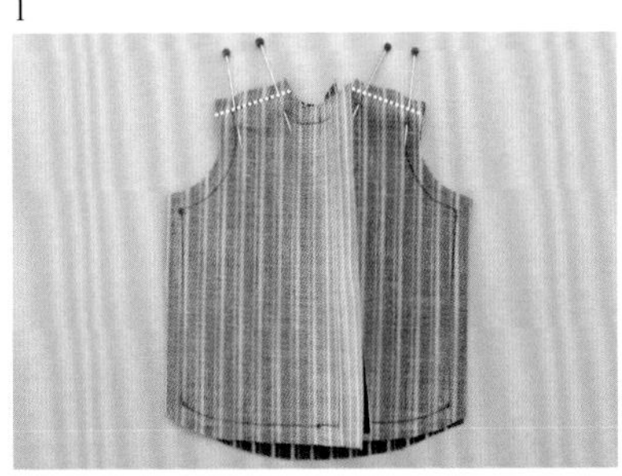

Arrange the templates on the fabric and cut out all the sections, then apply fray stopper liquid to the edges. With the right sides of the front and back bodice sections facing, sew the shoulders.

2

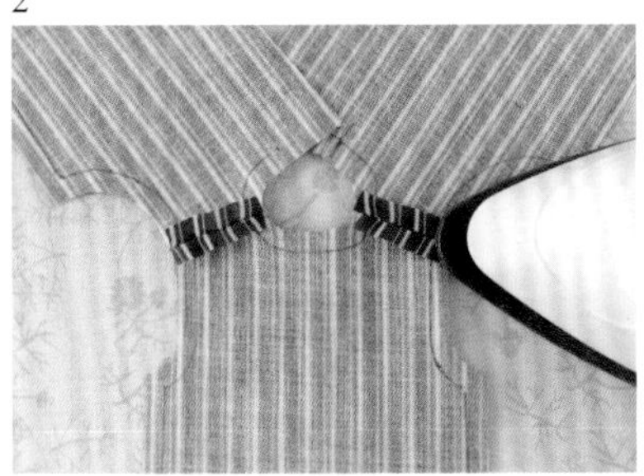

Iron open the seam allowances.

3

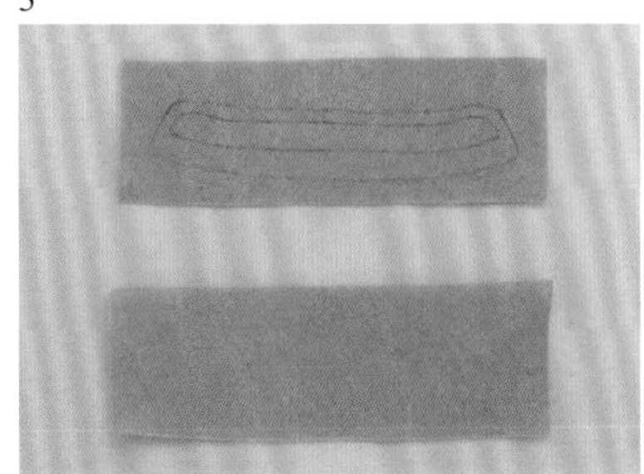

Trace the collar template on to the fabric and cut widely around it. Prepare another piece of fabric the same size.

4

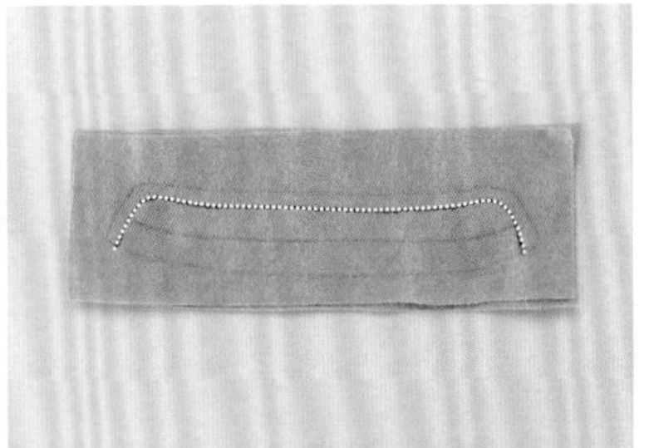

Place the two pieces of fabric together with right sides facing and sew along the outer seam line.

5

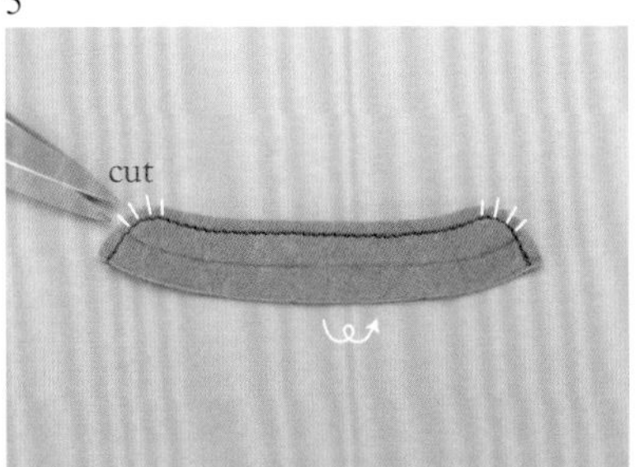


Cut the collar sections out, leaving the seam allowances, and cut fine slits in the curves.

6

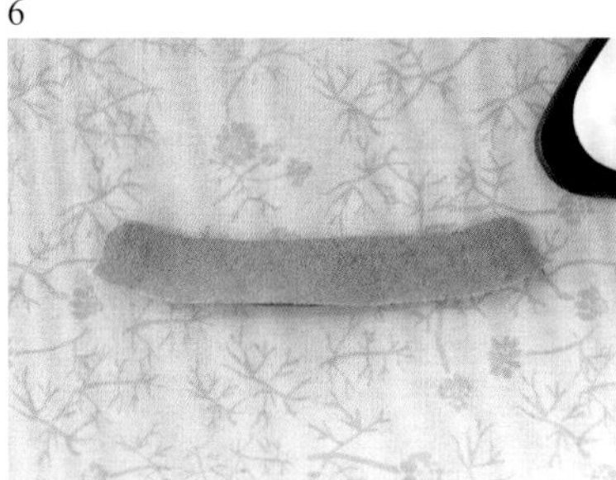

Turn the piece the right side out, using a tailor's awl to neatly push out the corners and curves, then iron to shape.

7

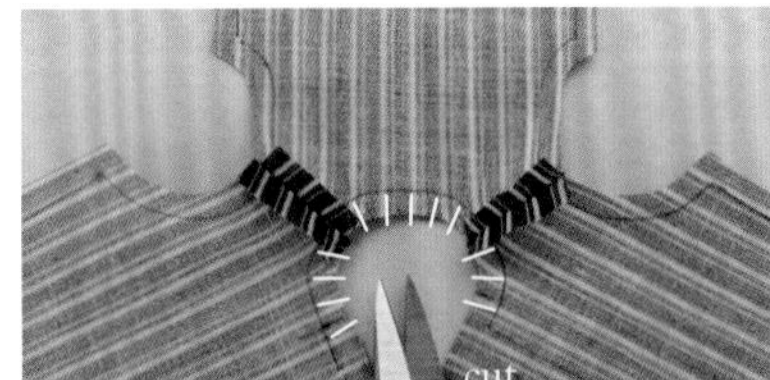


Cut fine slits into the seam allowance of the bodice neckline.

8

Apply fabric glue to the seam allowance and place the collar on top.

9

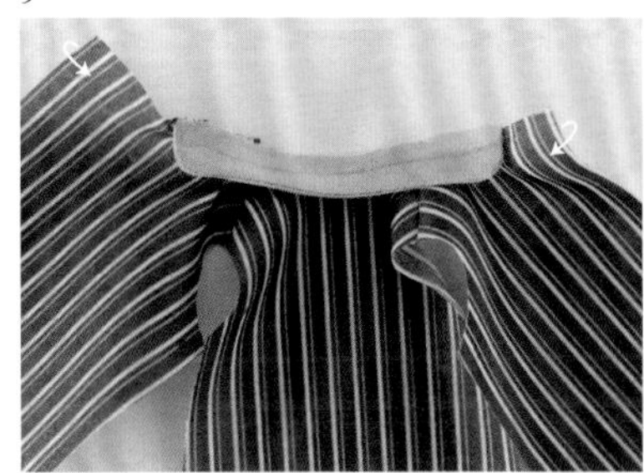

Fold the front facing so it faces inwards.

10

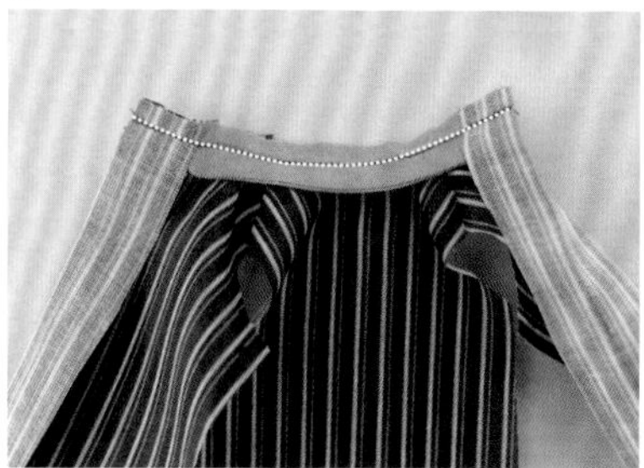

Sew the neckline.

11

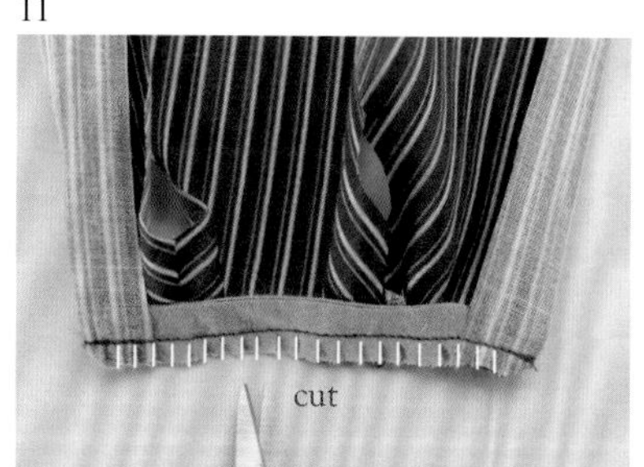


Cut fine slits into the seam allowance of the collar.

12

Turn the front facing the right side out, stand the collar up, then iron to shape.

13

Sew reinforced stitches from the front opening hem where the front facing is folded to the base of the collar on the bodice.

14

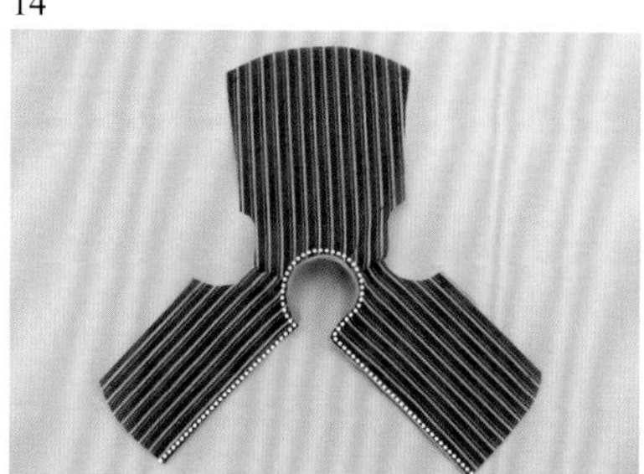

Sew from one side of the front opening around the neckline down the other side of the front opening.

15

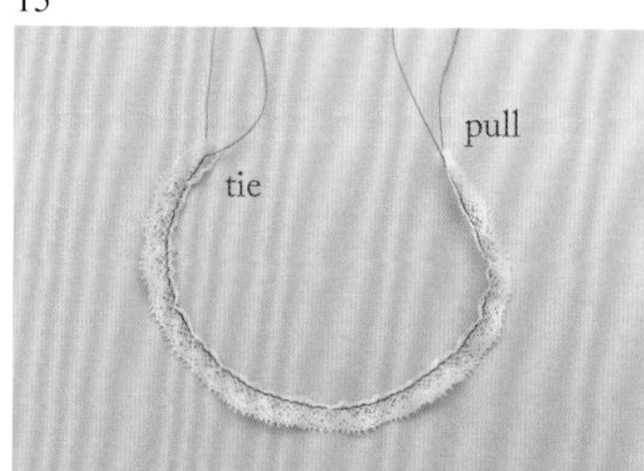


Prepare the lace for the collar. Machine sew one line of gathering stitches 2.5 mm (0.1 in) in length along the straight edge (not the curved side) of the lace (refer to p. 92).

16

Gather the lace to match the width where it will be attached around the collar and down the front of the shirt and iron to shape.

17

Temporarily fix the lace with fabric glue.

18

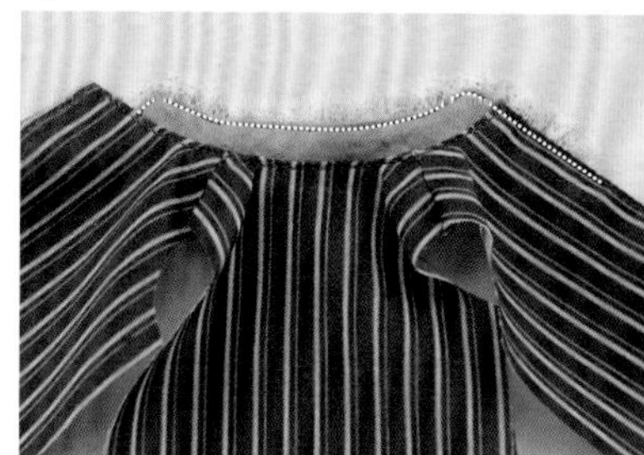

Sew the lace in place.

19

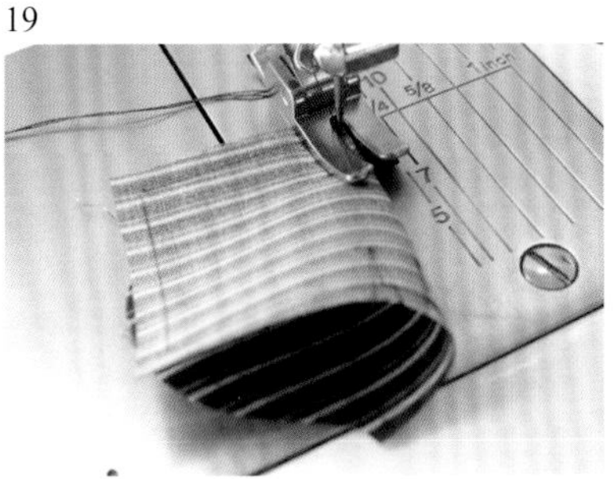

Create the darts one by one. Fold the fabric to face right side in and sew. Repeat to make four darts.

20

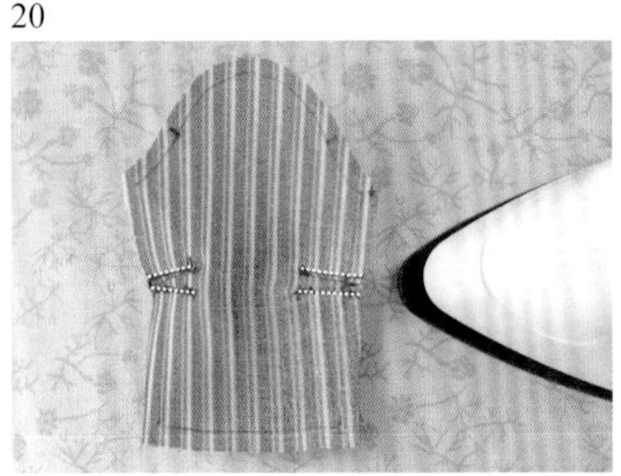

Fold the seam allowances of each dart inward and iron flat.

21

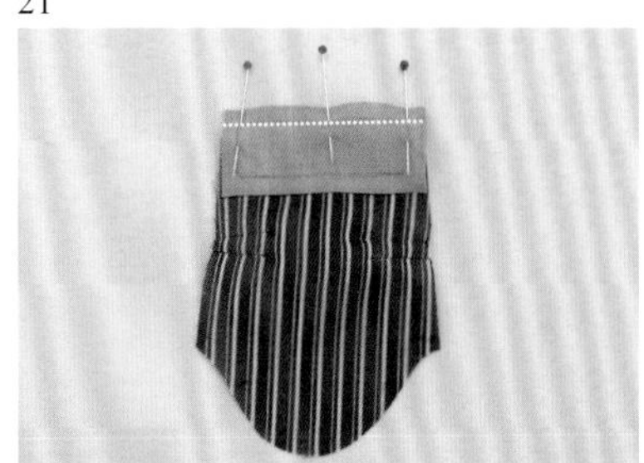

(*For size L, please skip to step 34 for how to arrange the sleeve opening.)

With right sides facing, sew the cuffs to the sleeve openings.

22

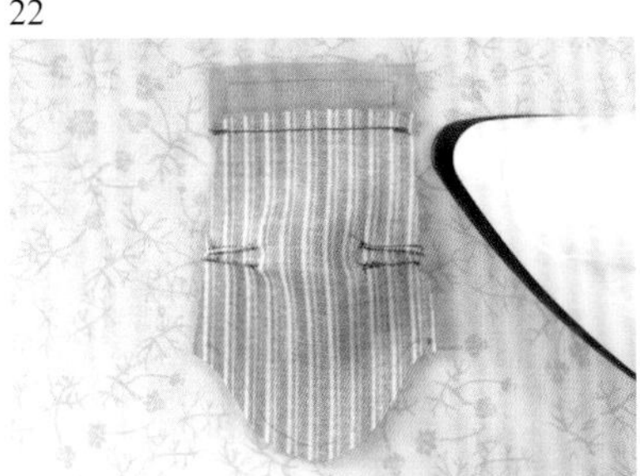

Fold the seam allowance toward the cuffs and fold the cuffs over.

23

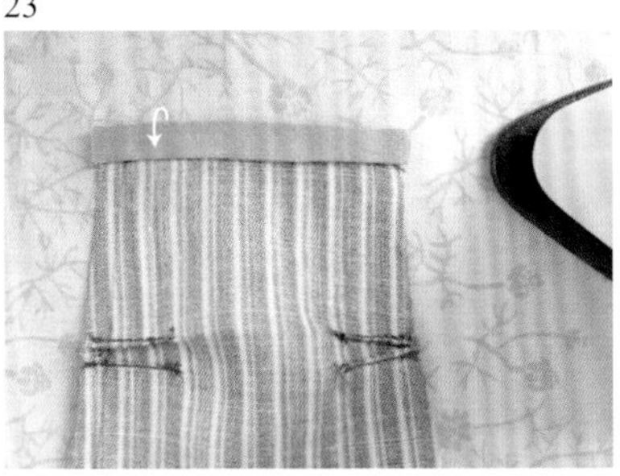

Use an iron to double-fold the cuffs so they wrap around the seam allowance.

24

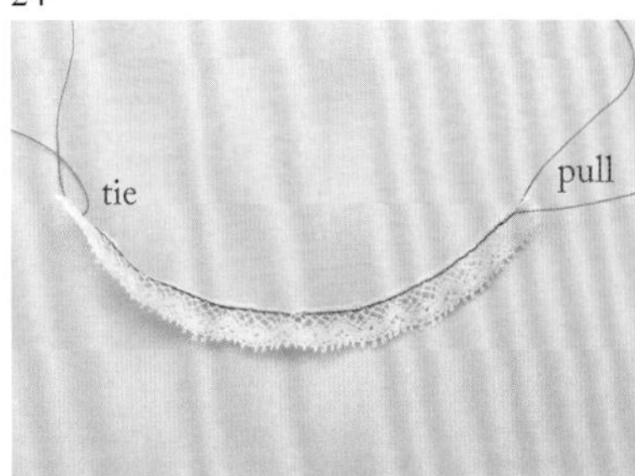


Prepare the lace for the sleeve openings. Machine sew one line of gathering stitches 2.5 mm (0.1 in) in length along the straight edge of the lace.

25

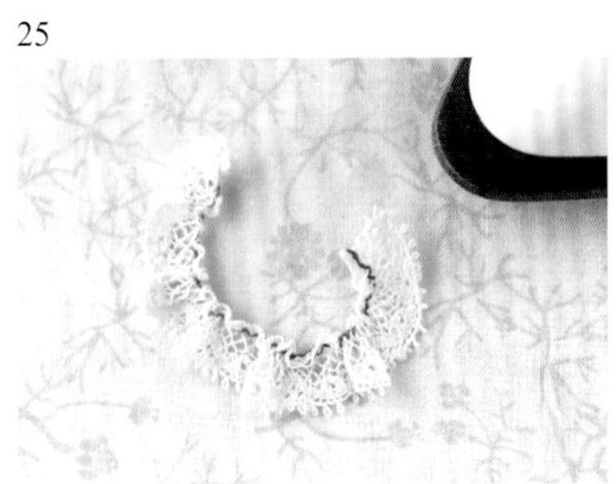

Gather the lace to match the width of the cuffs and iron to shape.

26

Temporarily fix the lace with fabric glue.

27

Sew the lace in place, then sew reinforced stitches all around the cuffs.

28

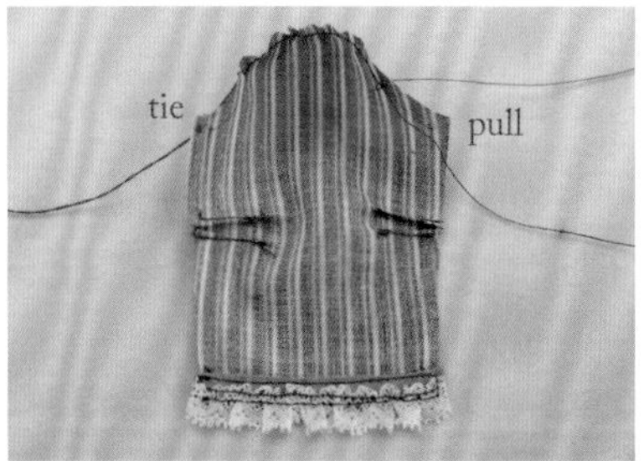


Machine sew one line of gathering stitches 2.5 mm (0.1 in) in length in the sleeve cap seam allowances from marker to marker. Then gather the fabric to match the width of the bodice armholes (refer to p. 92).

29

With right sides facing, sew the front bodice armholes and the sleeve caps together. Place the seam allowance toward the sleeves and iron flat.

30

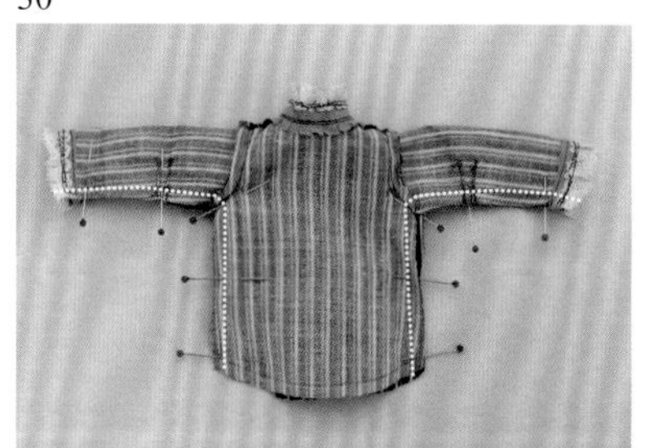

With the right sides of the front and back bodice sections facing, sew them together from the sleeve openings along under the arms and down to the hem.

31

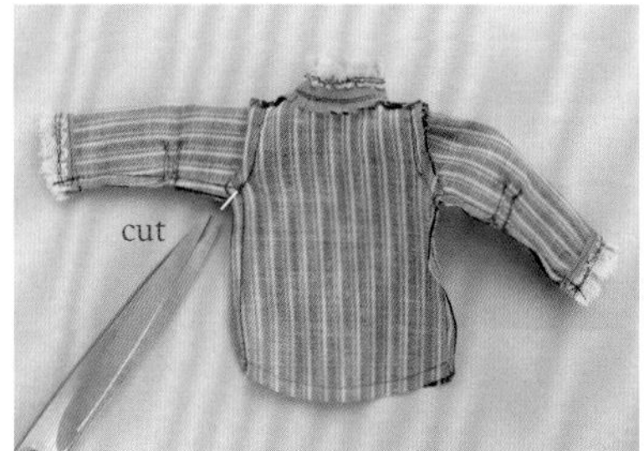


Cut slits into the seam allowance under the arms. Turn the piece right side out and iron open the seam allowance.

32

Fold and iron the seam allowance of the hem inward and sew.

33

Add snaps to the front opening and attach buttons to the cuffs. Size S and M are now complete.

34

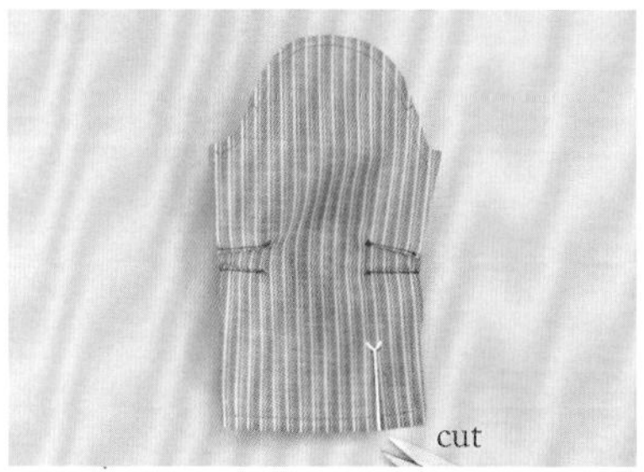


For size L, make side openings on the sleeves. Use the template to cut side openings into the left and right sleeve openings.

35

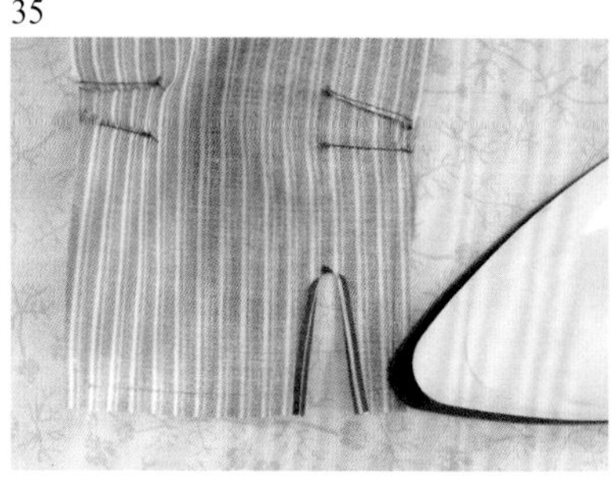

Fold the edges of the side openings inward by 2 mm (0.08 in) and iron flat.

36

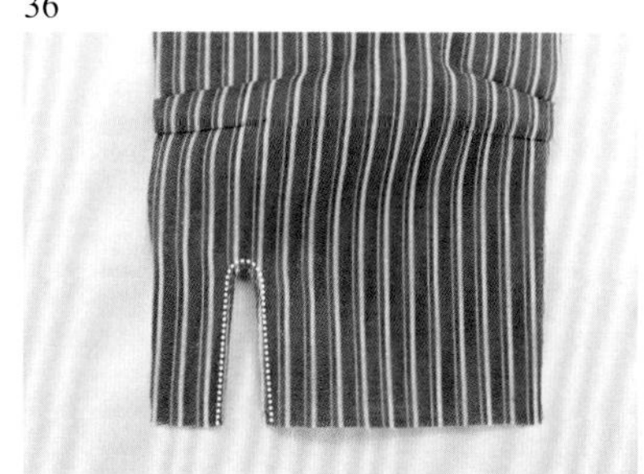

Sew around the side openings.

37

With right sides facing, sew a 2 cm (0.8 in) line in length from the sleeve opening.

38

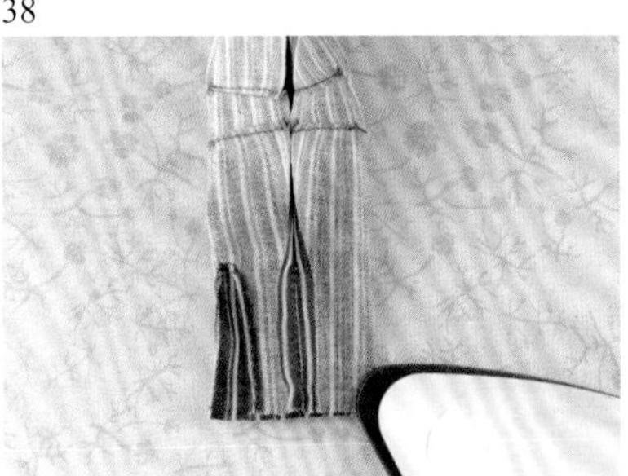

Iron open the seam allowances.

39

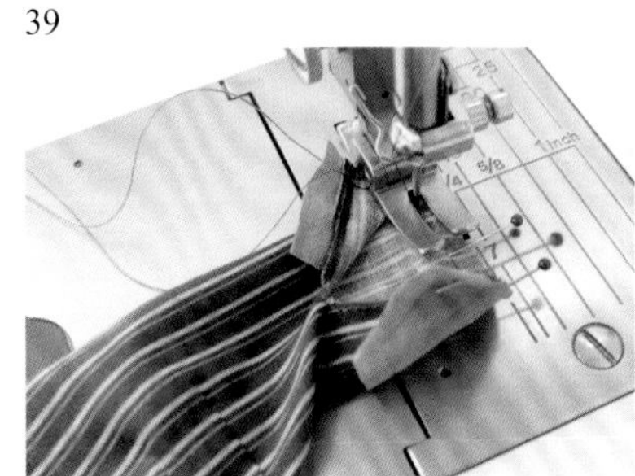

Turn the sleeve the right side out, then place one of the cuffs on the sleeve opening with right sides facing and sew together.

40

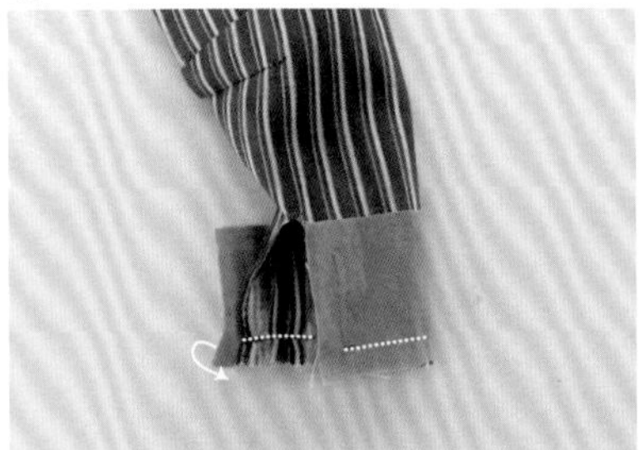

Turn the cuff inward.

41

Place the other cuff on the first cuff with right sides facing and sew together, then cut the corners of the seam allowance.

42

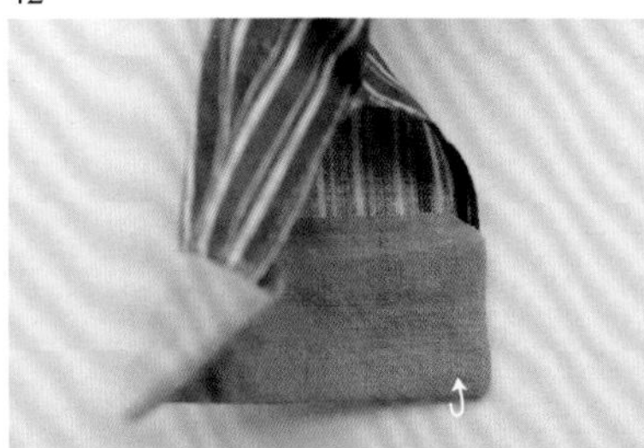

Turn the cuff the right side out and iron to shape.

43

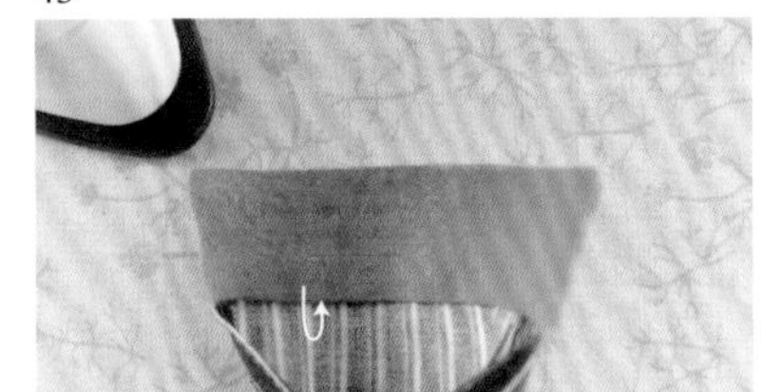

Fold and iron the seam allowance inwards, then iron to shape.

44

Gather the lace for the sleeve opening and temporarily fix it to the cuff. Then sew it in place and add reinforced stitches all around the cuff.

45

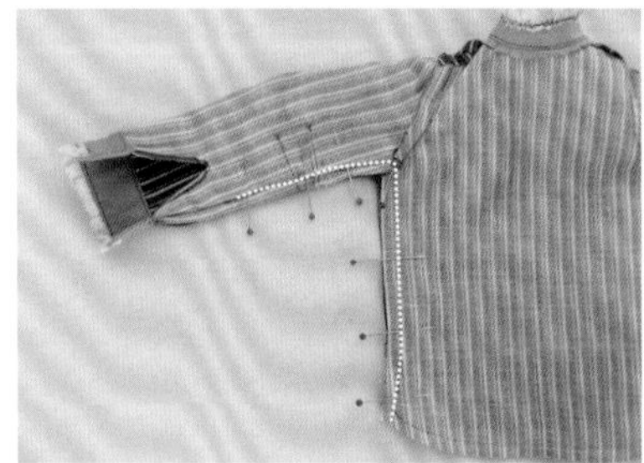

Turn the sleeve inside out and with the right sides of the front and back bodice sections facing, sew together from the sleeve openings along under the arms and down to the hem. To complete the piece, add snaps and decorative buttons.

# Skirt

This skirt with lovely volume and a gathered waist is great for beginners.
You will find yourself wanting to make it in red, ecru, black, and all the basic wardrobe colors.

| | | | | | |
|---|---|---|---|---|---|
| Cotton linen | S 38 × 15 cm (15 × 5.9 in) | 4 mm (0.16 in) buttons | S, M 2 pieces | L 4 pieces |
| | M 40 × 20 cm (15.7 × 7.9 in) | | | |
| | L 90 × 30 cm (35.4 × 11.8 in) | Snaps | 2 pairs | |

1

Arrange the paper templates on the fabric and cut out all the sections, then apply fray stopper liquid to the edges. With the right sides of the skirt sections facing, sew one side together.

2

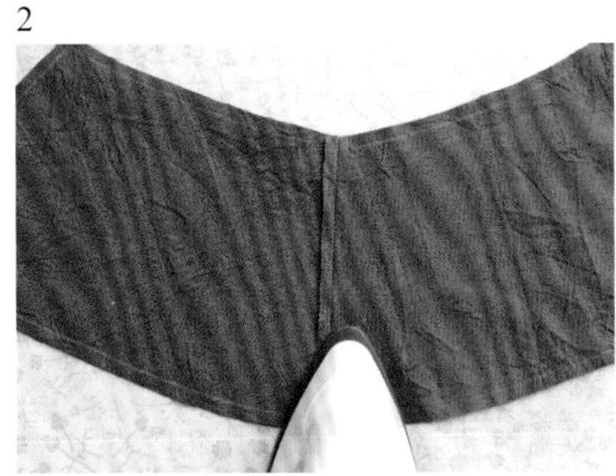

Iron open the seam allowances.

3

With the right sides of the front and back yoke waistbands facing, sew them together. Make two—one for the front and one for the back of the skirt.

4

Iron open the seam allowances.

5

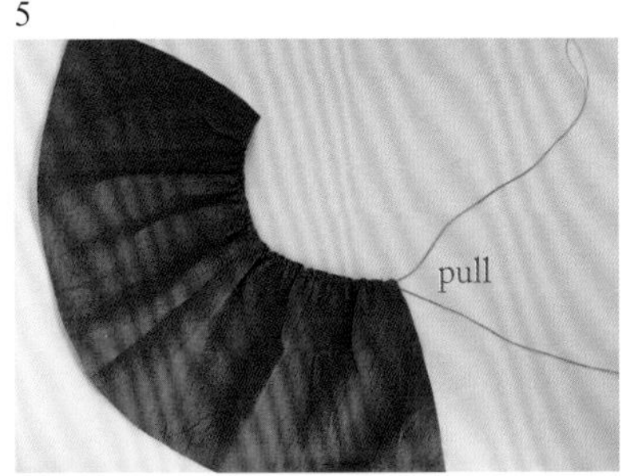


Machine sew two lines of gathering stitches 3 mm (0.12 in) in length in the skirt waist seam allowance (refer to p. 92).

6

Gather the fabric to match the width of the yoke waistband and iron to shape.

7

Place the skirt and yoke waistband so the right sides are facing, then fold the seam allowance of one side of the skirt (the back yoke waistband side) inward.

8

Sew the skirt and yoke waistband together with right sides facing.

9

Place the seam allowance up and iron flat.

10

Place the second yoke waistband on top of the first with right sides facing and sew together.

11

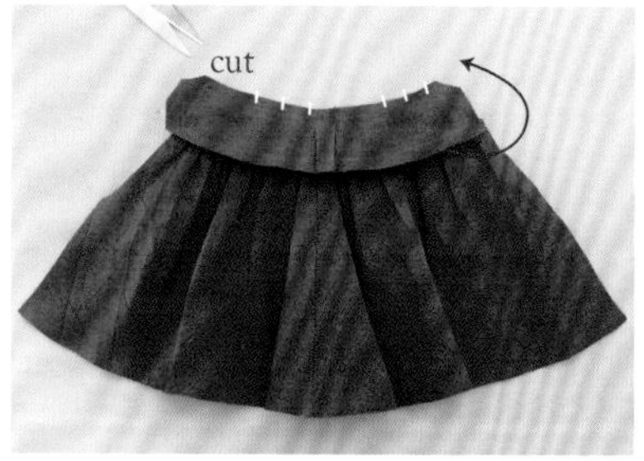


Cut the corners of the seam allowances and cut slits. Turn the yoke waistband inward.

12

Place the yoke waistband seam allowance inward and iron flat. Then fold the edges of the skirt opening diagonally to slightly below the opening stop marker.

13

Sew reinforced stitches on the yoke waistband. Sew the opening of the back yoke waistband.

14

Fold the seam allowance of the skirt hem inward and iron flat.

15

Sew the skirt hem.

16

With right sides facing, sew up the side from the skirt hem to the opening stop marker.

17

Iron open the seam allowances.

18

Rinse the skirt in water and leave to dry naturally. Then add snaps and attach decorative buttons to complete the piece.

# Waistcoat & Corsage

This winter waistcoat can be made with cotton and linen for use in other seasons.
When you need some extra flair, add the corsage.

| | | | |
|---|---|---|---|
| Fine wale corduroy | S 16 × 12 cm (6.3 × 4.7 in)<br>M 22 × 15 cm (8.7 × 5.9 in)<br>L 30 × 20 cm (11.8 × 7.9 in) | Cotton lawn | S 16 × 10 cm (6.3 × 3.9 in)<br>M 22 × 10 cm (8.7 × 3.9 in)<br>L 30 × 18 cm (11.8 × 7.1 in) |
| 2.5 mm (0.1 in) buttons | S, M 5 pieces<br>L 6 pieces | Hooks | S, M 2 pieces L 3 pieces |
| Paper-covered wire | | Insect pins | |

1

With the right sides of the front and back bodice outer fabric facing, sew the shoulders.

2

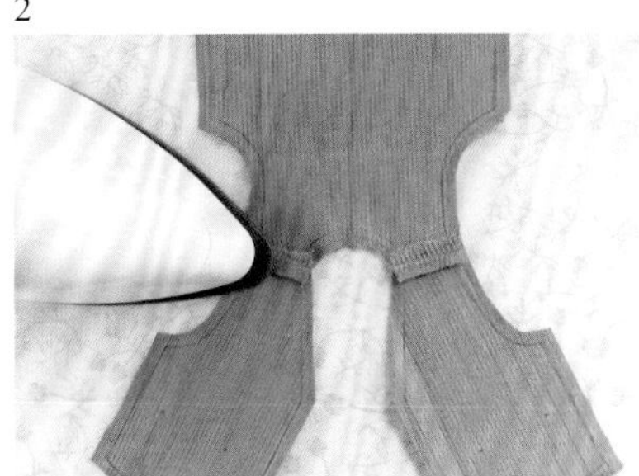

Iron open the seam allowances.

3

Do the same with inner lining, and with the right sides of the front and back bodice sections facing, sew at the shoulders.

4

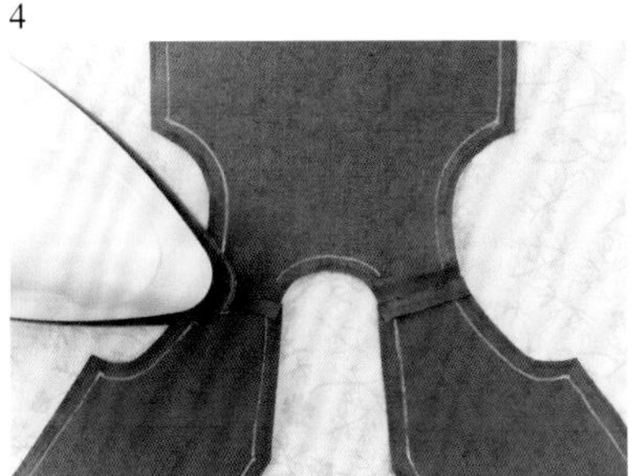

Iron open the seam allowances.

5

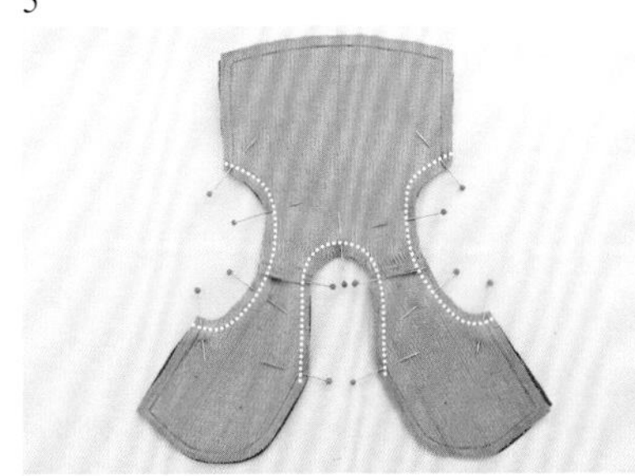

With the right sides of the outer fabric and inner lining facing, sew the neckline and sleeve openings.

6

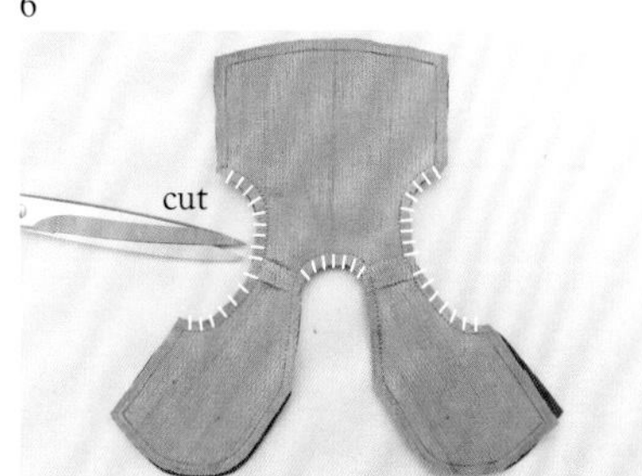


Cut fine slits into the seam allowance.

7

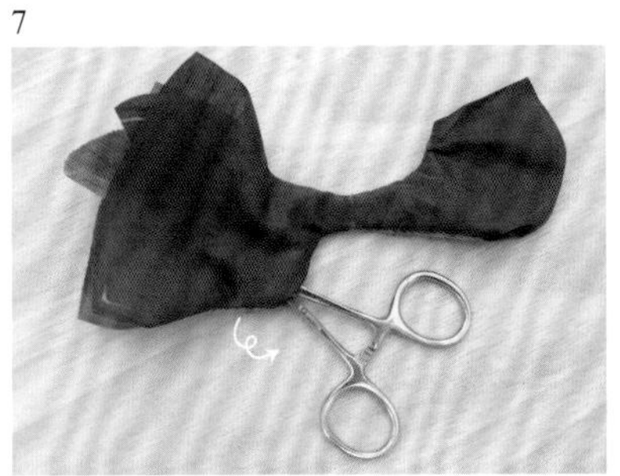

Use tweezers or similar tool to turn the piece the right side out.

8

Use a tailor's awl to neatly push out the corners and curves, then iron to shape.

9

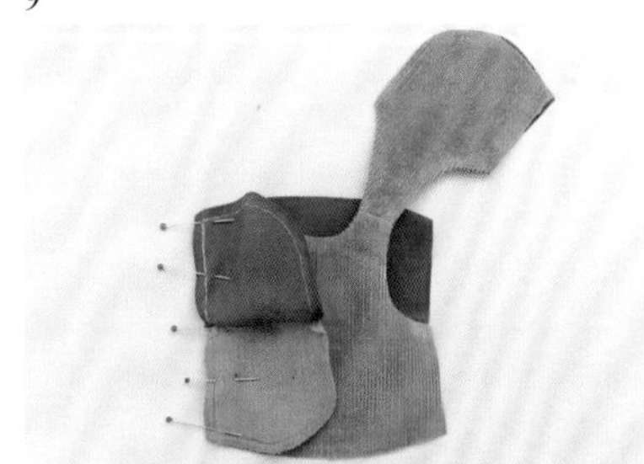

With the right sides of the front and back bodice outer fabric facing and the section sides aligned, hold in place with marking pins. Do the same with the front and back bodice inner lining.

10

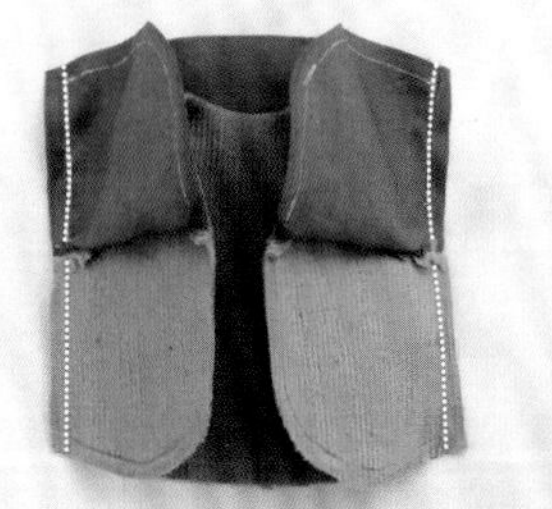

Sew the sides of both the outer fabric and the inner lining sections.

11

Iron open the seam allowances on the sides of both the outer fabric and inner lining. Then with the right sides facing, hold in place with marking pins from the front opening to the hem.

12

Leaving a seam opening in the hem, sew from the left and right front openings down to the hem.

13

Cut the corners of the seam allowances, cutting slits where the fabric curves.

14

Use tweezers or similar tool to turn the piece the right side out through the seam opening. Use a tailor's awl to neatly push out the corners and curves, then iron to shape.

15

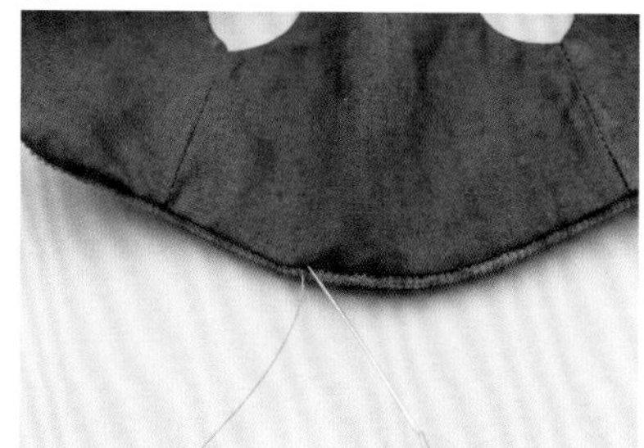

Close up the seam opening with blind stitches.

16

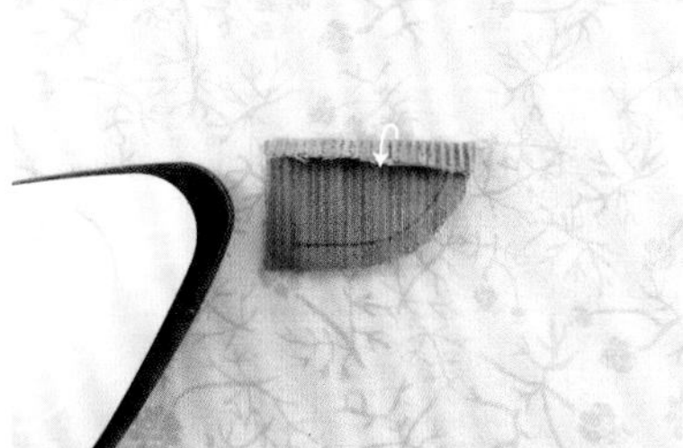

Fold the seam allowance of the top of the pocket and iron flat.

17

Sew the top of the pocket.

18

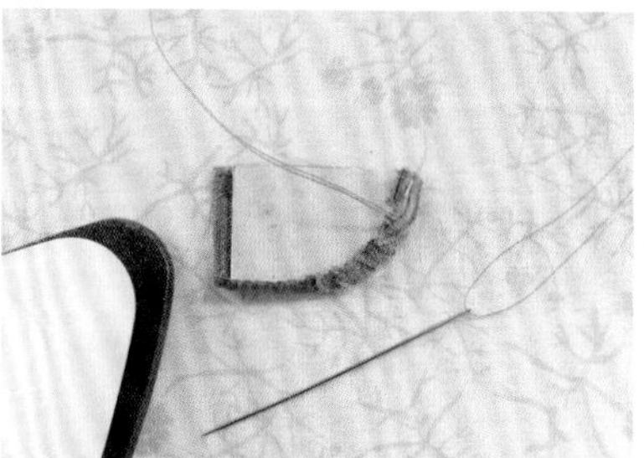

Sew running stitches 3 mm (0.12 in) in length on the curved sections of the pocket. Then pull the stitches to gather the fabric so it aligns with the template and forms curves, then iron the seam allowances flat.

19

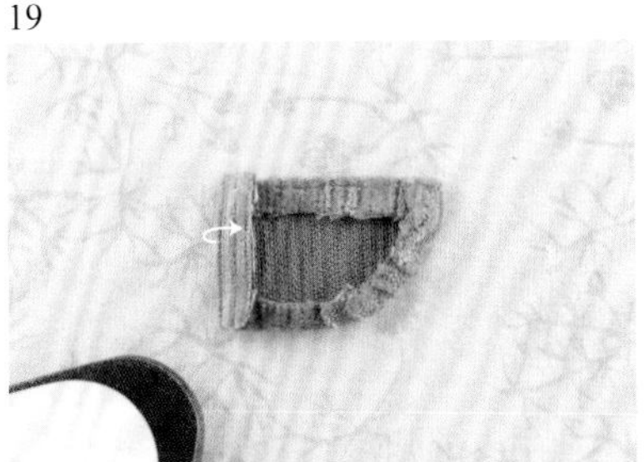

Fold the seam allowance on the other side too and iron in place.

20

Apply fabric glue to the pocket seam allowances, temporarily fix the pockets in place on the bodice, then sew.

21

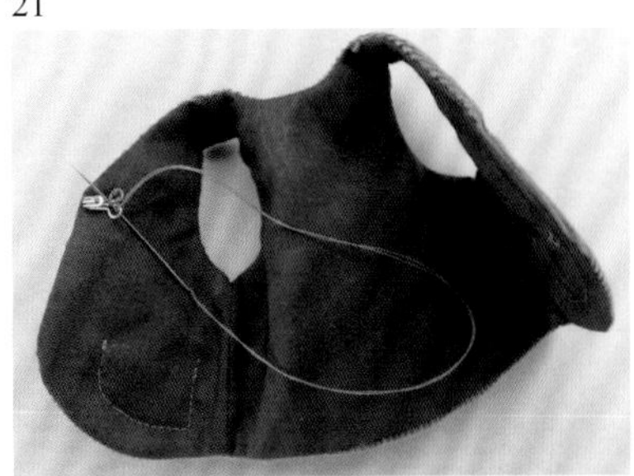

Attach a hook on the front opening and create a loop with thread on the opposite side (refer to p. 93).

22

Add decorative buttons to complete the waistcoat.

23

Use scraps of the outer fabric to make a corsage. Cut three 1 cm (0.4 in) squares. Prepare 3 cm (1.2 in) of floral stem paper-covered wire.

24

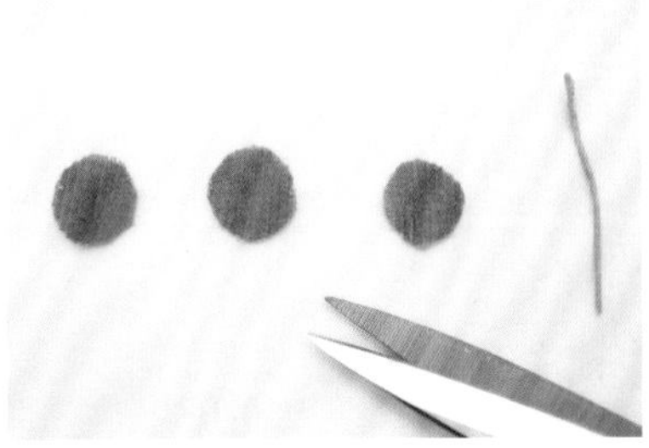

Cut the corners and apply fray stopper liquid to the edges.

25

Layer the three pieces and sew them together in the center.

26

Fold the wire in half and sew in place on the back.

27

Scrunch up the fabric and sew either an insect pin or safety pin on the back to complete the corsage.

# Trousers

These trousers pair up with the waistcoat.
Try making them in cotton or linen and rinse them in water to give a natural finished look.

| | | |
|---|---|---|
| Fine wale corduroy | S | 20 × 18 cm (7.9 × 7.1 in) |
| | M | 30 × 25 cm (11.8 × 9.8 in) |
| | L | 40 × 35 cm (15.7 × 13.8 in) |
| Cotton lawn for the pocket lining | S | 6 × 3 cm (2.4 × 1.2 in) |
| | M | 8 × 5 cm (3.1 × 2 in) |
| | L | 10 × 7 cm (3.9 × 2.8 in) |
| Snaps | S, M | 1 pair |
| | L | 2 pairs |

1

Cut out the sections and apply fray stopper liquid to the edges. Place the pocket lining on the front pocket opening with right sides facing and sew them together at the opening.

2

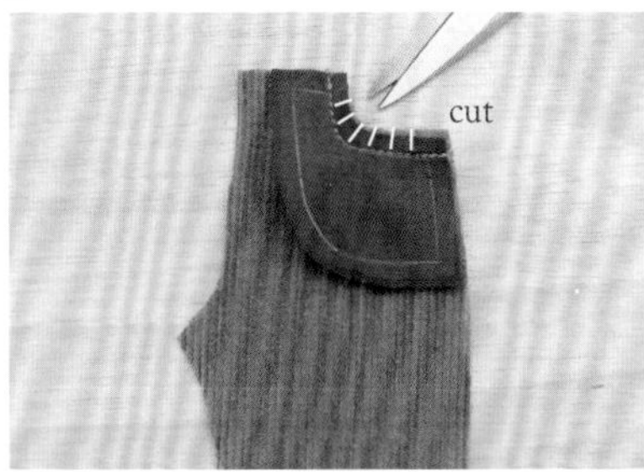


Cut slits into the seam allowance.

3

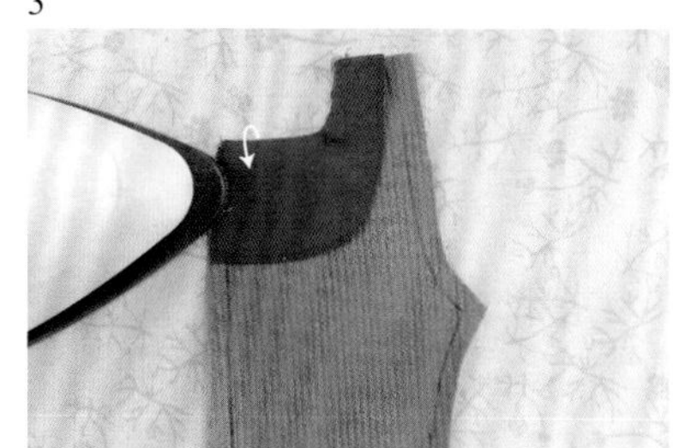

Turn the pocket lining over to the back, then iron to shape.

4

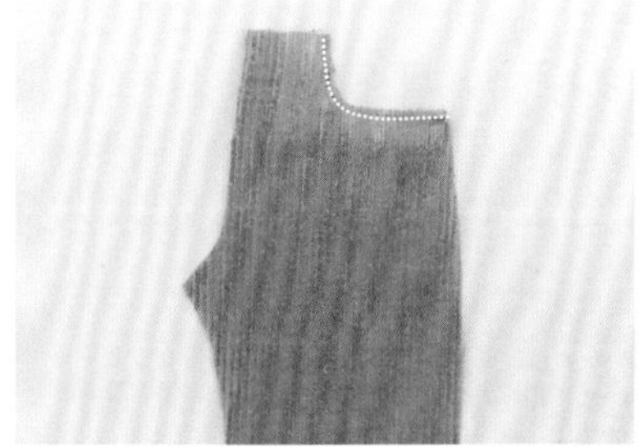

Sew reinforced stitches along the top of the pocket.

5

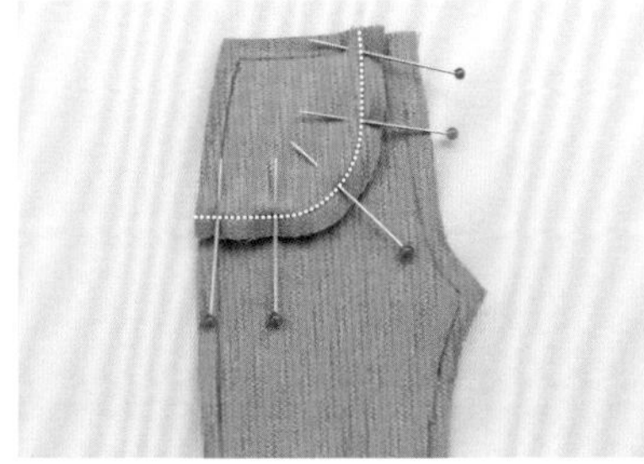

Place the pocket side fabric on the pocket lining and sew together.

6

Be careful not to sew it to the trousers underneath.

7

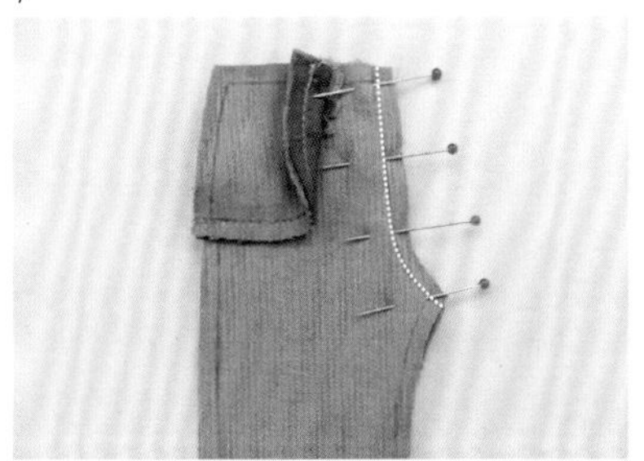

With the right sides of the left and right front trouser sections facing, sew the front rise.

8

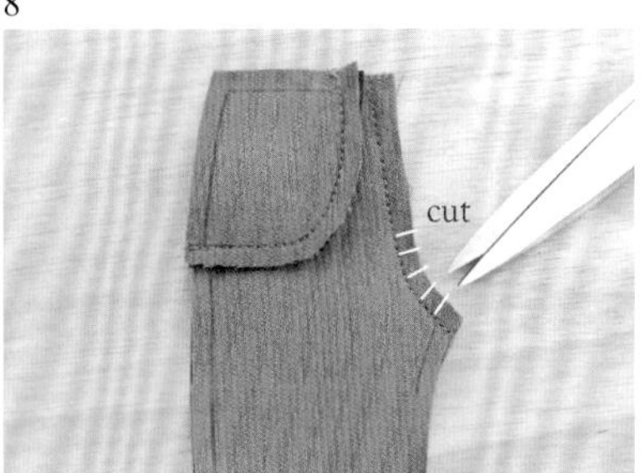


Cut slits in the seam allowances where the fabric curves.

9

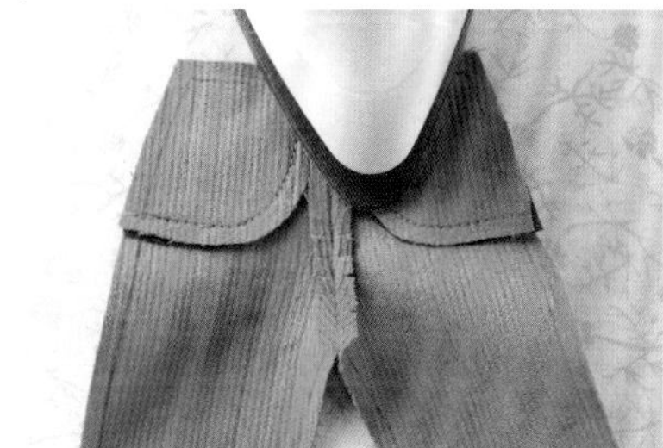

Iron open the seam allowances.

10

Sew reinforced stitches on left and right front rise sections, then sew additional stitching on the left.

11

With the right sides of the front and back trouser sections facing, sew the side edges.

12

Iron open the seam allowances.

13

Sew reinforced stitches on the left and right side edges.

14

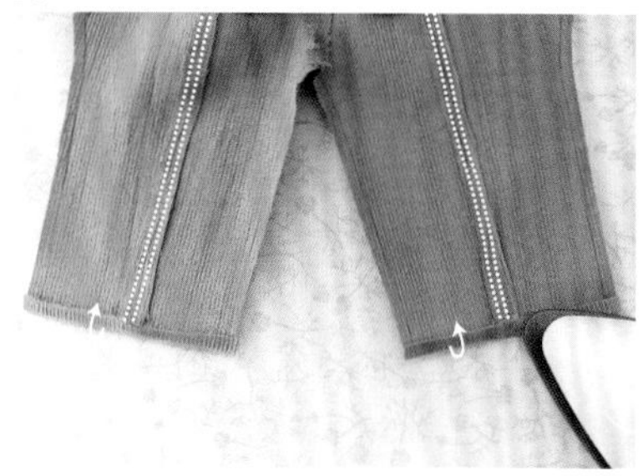

Fold the seam allowance of the hem inward using an iron.

15

Sew the hem.

16

With the right sides of the trousers and waist band facing, sew the waist. Place the seam allowance up.

17

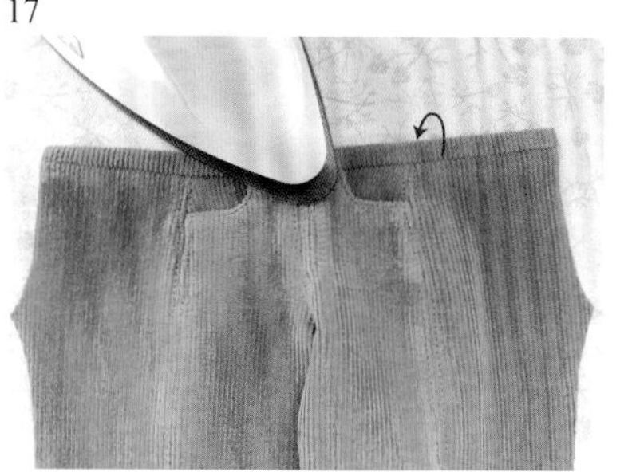

Use an iron to double-fold the waist band so it wraps around the seam allowance. If the fabric is thick, a single-fold is fine.

18

Sew reinforced stitches on the waist band section.

19

Looking from the back, cut a slit in the seam allowance at the opening stop marker on the back pant rise section.

20

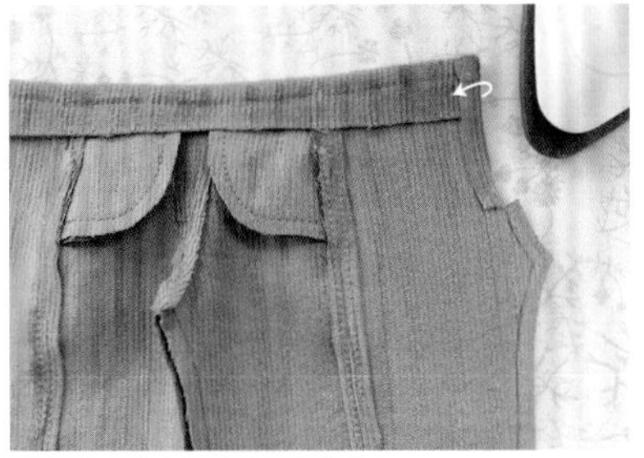

Fold the seam allowance of the back opening above the slit inwards and iron flat.

21

Sew the back opening.

22

Fold the seam allowances of the top of the back pockets and sew them.

23

Sew running stitches 3 mm (0.12 in) in length on the curved sections of the pocket. Pull the stitches to gather the fabric so it aligns with the template and forms curves, then iron the seam allowances flat.

24

Apply fabric glue to the pocket seam allowances, temporarily fix the pockets in place on the back trouser section, then sew.

25

With the right sides of the back trouser sections facing, sew the back rise to the opening stop marker. Iron open the seam allowances.

26

Sew the inseams together.

27

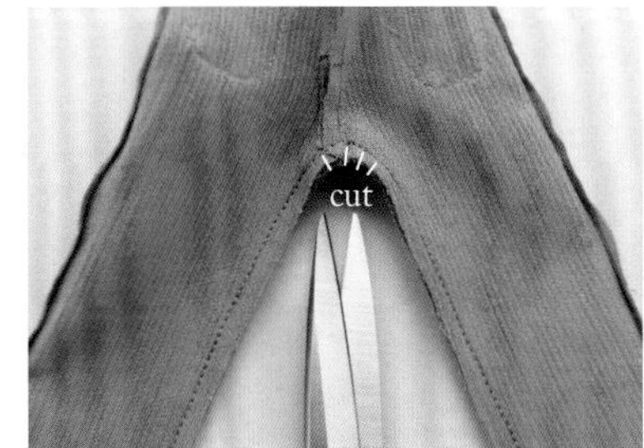


Cut slits into the seam allowance of the inseam and turn the right side out. Add snaps to the back opening to complete the trousers.

# Coat

This coat with its billowing style has a sweet look.
Make it in cotton or linen to match the season.

| | | | |
|---|---|---|---|
| Velvet | S 30 × 20 cm (11.8 × 7.9 in)<br>M 45 × 25 cm (17.7 × 9.8 in)<br>L 75 × 50 cm (29.5 × 19.7 in) | Cotton lawn for the lining | S 18 × 4 cm (7.1 × 1.6 in)<br>M 25 × 5 cm (9.8 × 2 in)<br>L 35 × 7 cm (13.8 × 2.8 in) |
| Hooks | S, M 3 pieces L 5 pieces | 4 mm (0.16 in) buttons | S, M 1 piece L 3 pieces |
| Snaps | L 2 pieces | | |

1

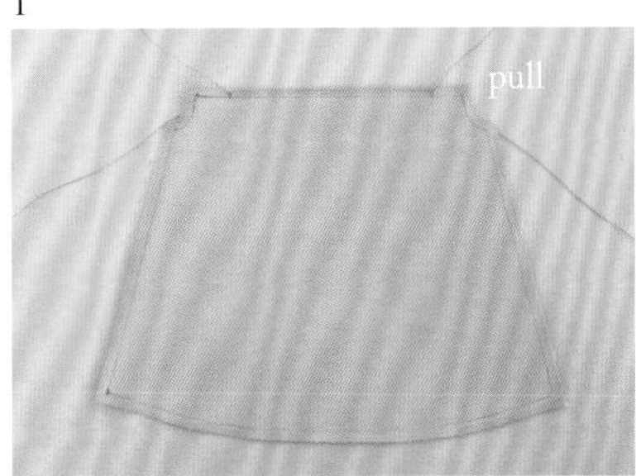


Apply fray stopper liquid to the edges of each section. Use a machine to sew two lines of gathering stitches 3 mm (0.12 in) in length in the seam allowance of the yoke of the back bodice from marker to marker.

2

Gather the fabric to match the width of the back yoke and iron to shape (refer to p. 92).

3

Sew the back bodice section and the yoke together with right sides facing.

4

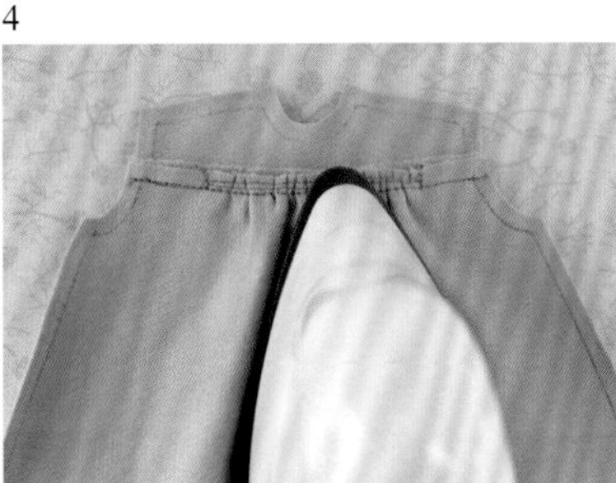

Place the seam allowance toward the yoke and iron flat.

5

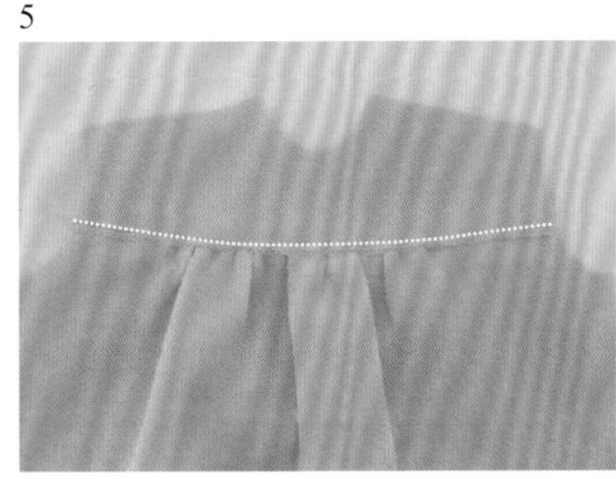

Sew reinforced stitches on the yoke.

6

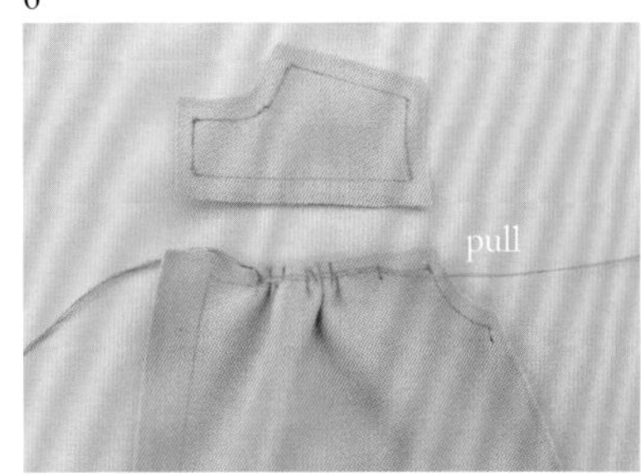


Use a machine to sew two lines of gathering stitches 3 mm (0.12 in) in length in the seam allowance of the front bodice yoke from marker to marker. Then gather the fabric to match the width of the front yoke section.

7

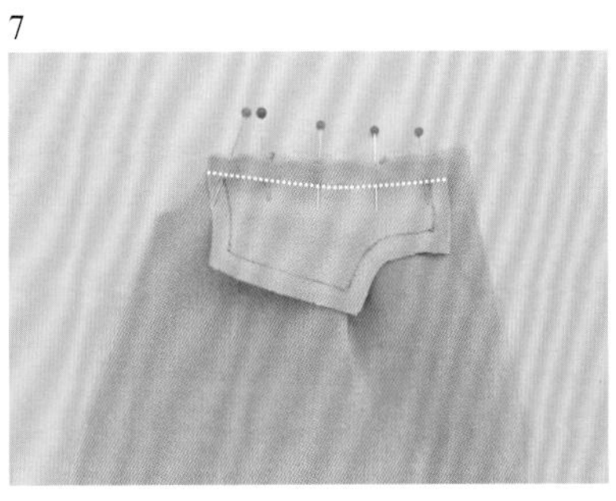

With right sides facing, sew the front bodice section and the front yoke together.

8

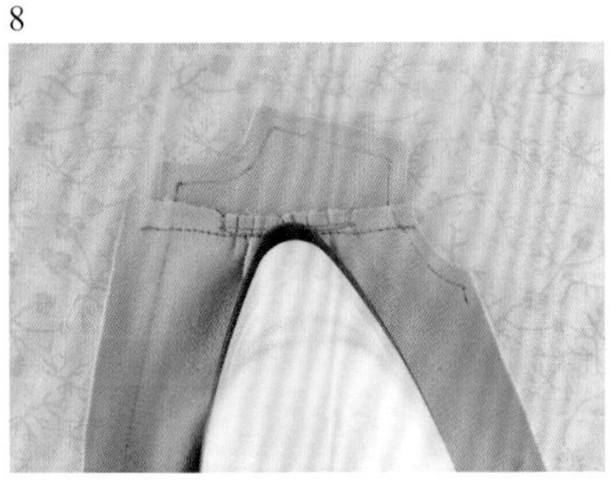

Place the seam allowance toward the yoke and iron flat.

9

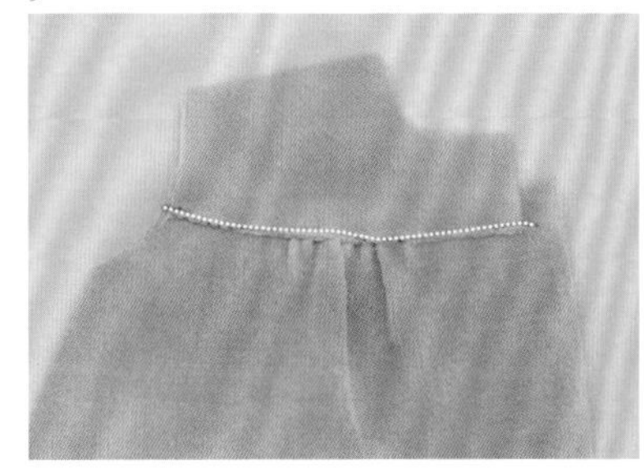

Sew reinforced stitches on the yoke.

10

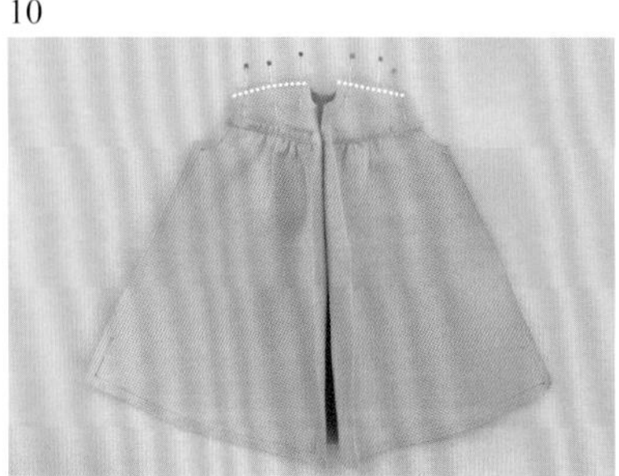

With the right sides of the front and back bodice sections facing, sew the shoulders.

11

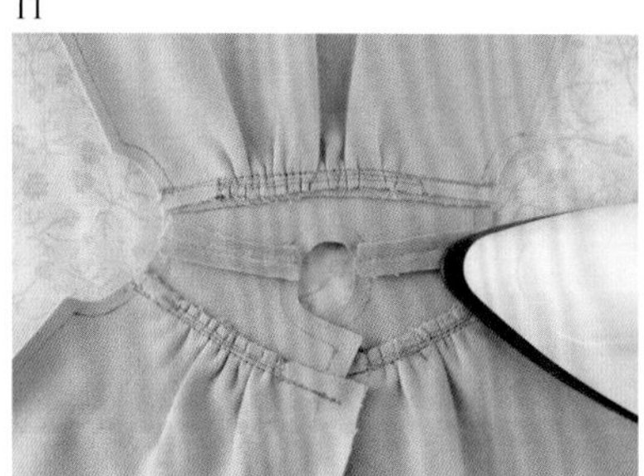

Iron open the seam allowances.

12

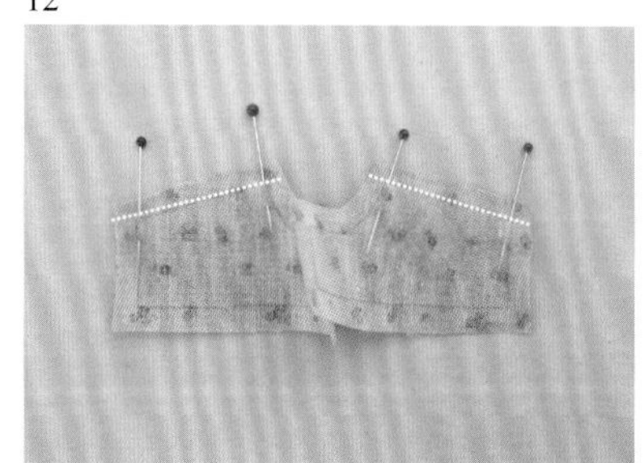

With the right sides of the front and back bodice inner lining facing, sew the shoulders.

13

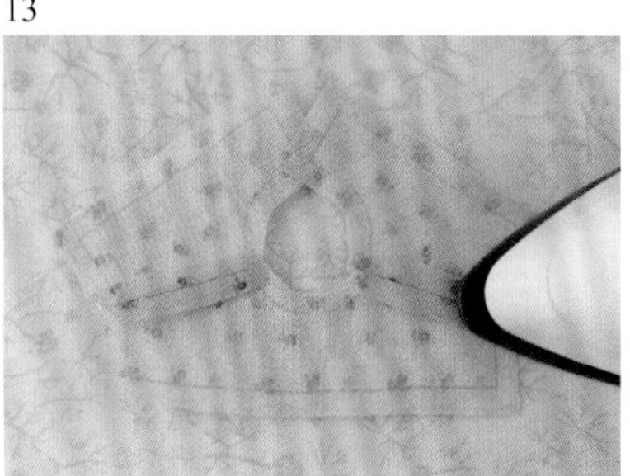

Iron open the seam allowances.

14

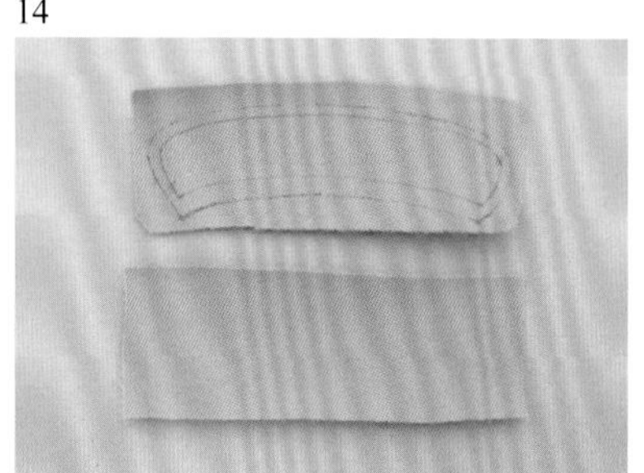

Trace the collar on to the fabric and cut widely around it. Prepare another piece of fabric the same size.

15

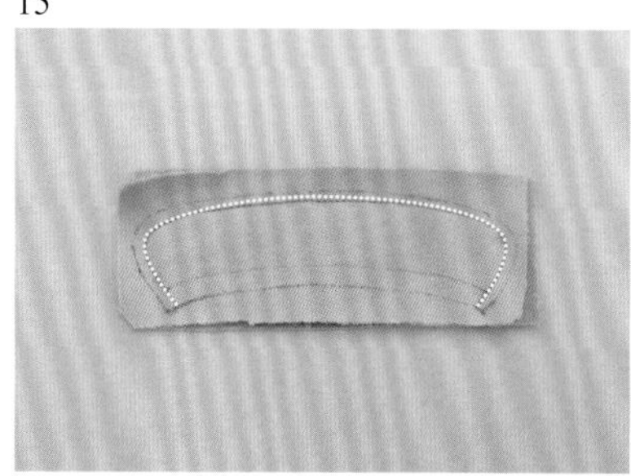

Place the two pieces of fabric together with right sides facing and sew along the outer seam line.

16

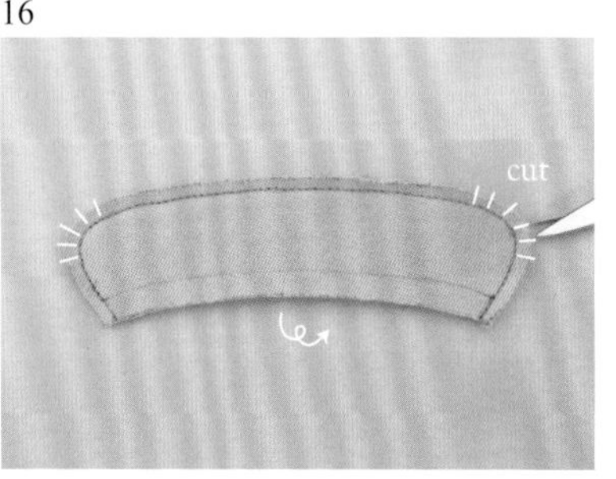


Cut the collar sections out, leaving the seam allowances, and cut fine slits in the curves.

17

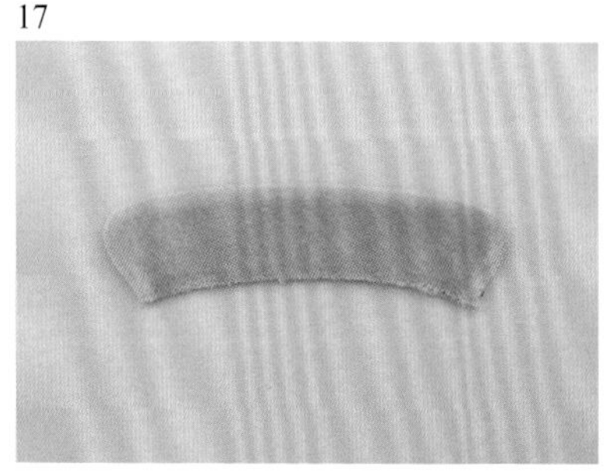

Turn the piece the right side out, using a tailor's awl to neatly push out the corners and curves, then iron to shape.

18

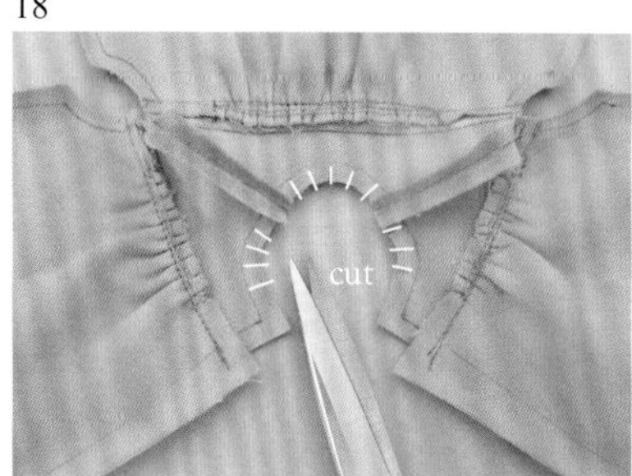


Cut fine slits into the seam allowance of the yoke neckline.

19

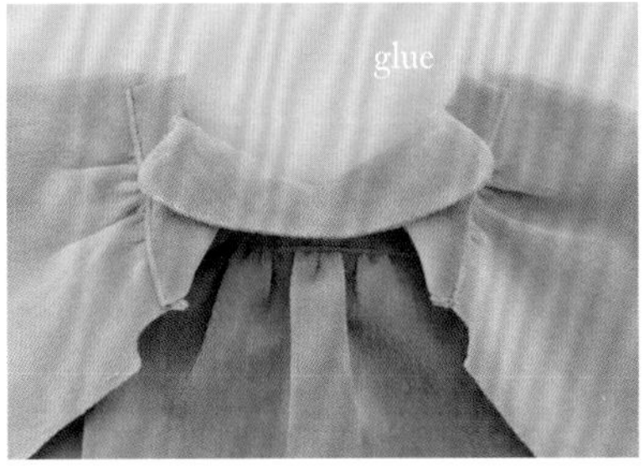


Apply fabric glue to the seam allowance and place the collar on top, right sides facing, to temporarily fix it in place.

20

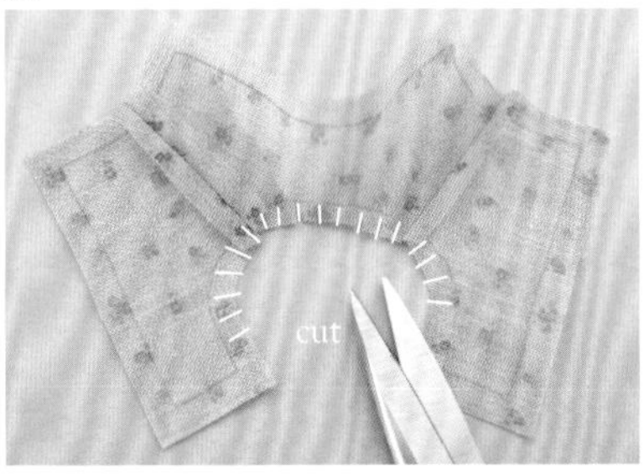


Cut fine slits into the seam allowance of the lining neckline.

21

With the right sides of the yoke and inner lining facing, temporarily fix in place with fabric glue, then machine sew together from the front opening to the neckline. Cut slits into the seam allowance of the collar and turn the right side out.

22

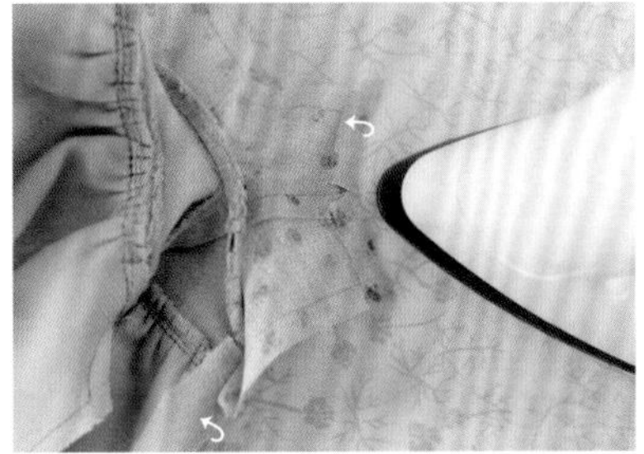

With an iron, fold the front facing of the bodice. Place the seam allowances of the lining armholes inward and iron flat.

23

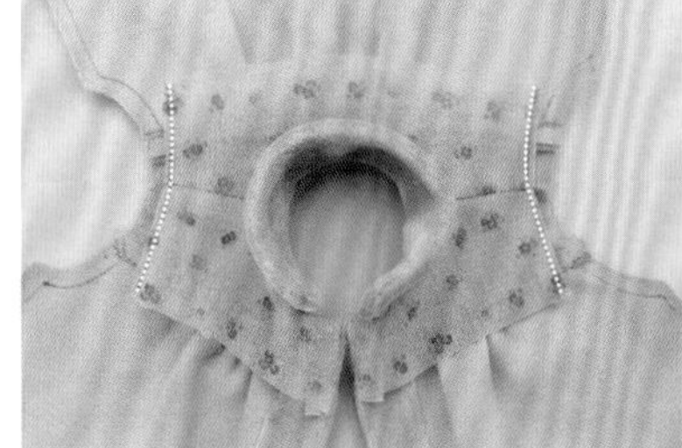

Sew the lining armholes (be careful not to sew it together with the yoke underneath).

24

For size L only, cut slits in the sleeve opening, then follow steps 34–38 on pp. 62–63 in the same way as for the blouse. Add gathering stitches to the sleeve opening.

25

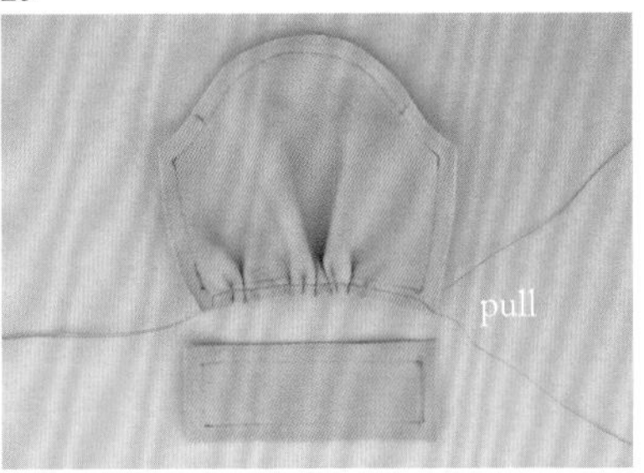


Use a machine to sew one line of gathering stitches 3 mm (0.12 in) in length in the sleeve opening seam allowances. Then gather the fabric to match the width of the cuffs.

26

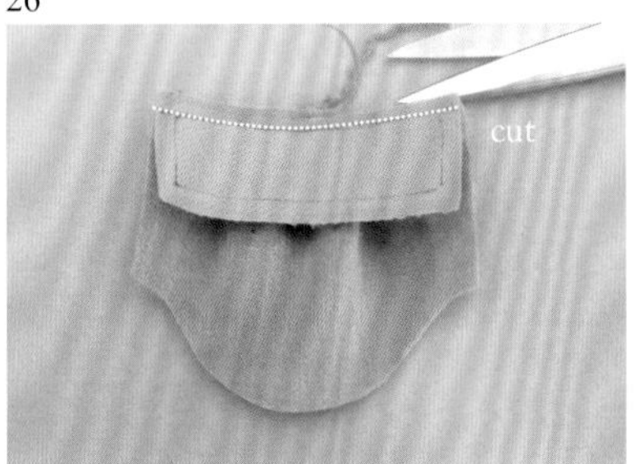


Sew the sleeve opening and the cuff together with right sides facing, then cut the seam allowance to 3 mm (0.12 in) in width.

27

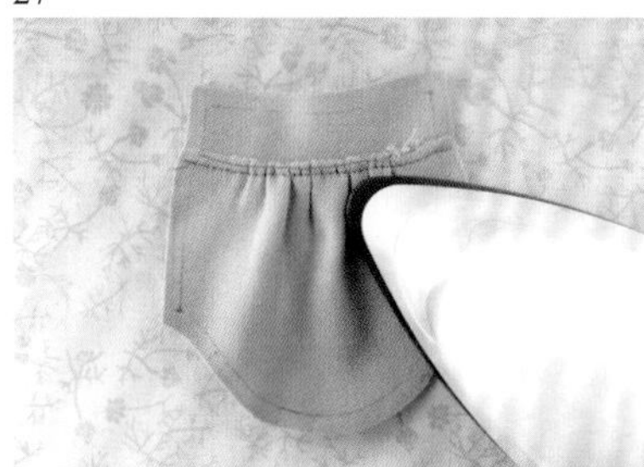

Fold the seam allowance toward the cuffs and fold the cuffs over.

28

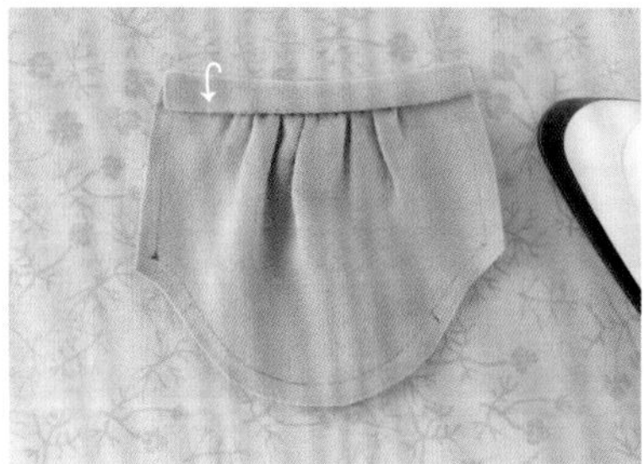

Use an iron to double-fold the cuffs so they wrap around the seam allowance.

29

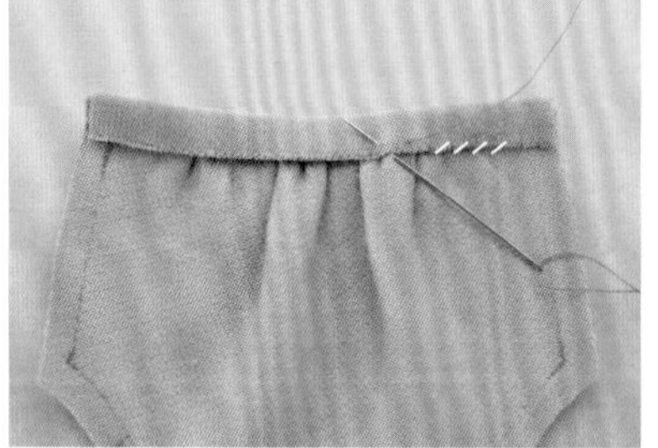

Sew the cuff hems with blind stitches to close them up.

30

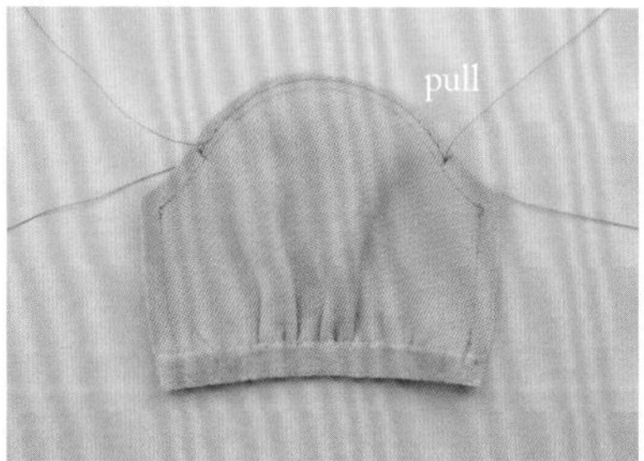


Use a machine to sew one line of gathering stitches 3 mm (0.12 in) in length in the sleeve cap seam allowances from marker to marker.

31

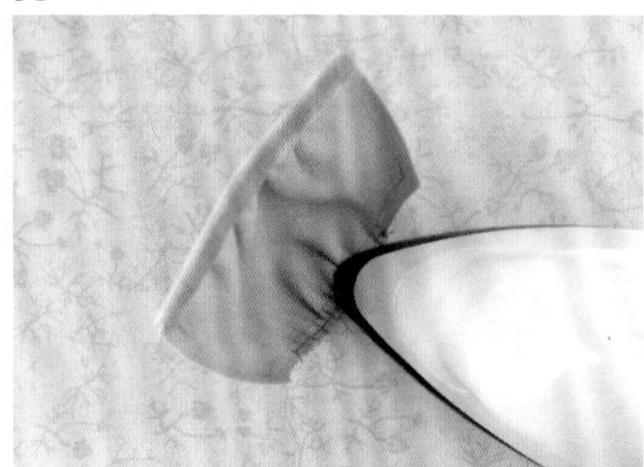

Gather the fabric to match the width of the bodice armholes and iron to shape.

32

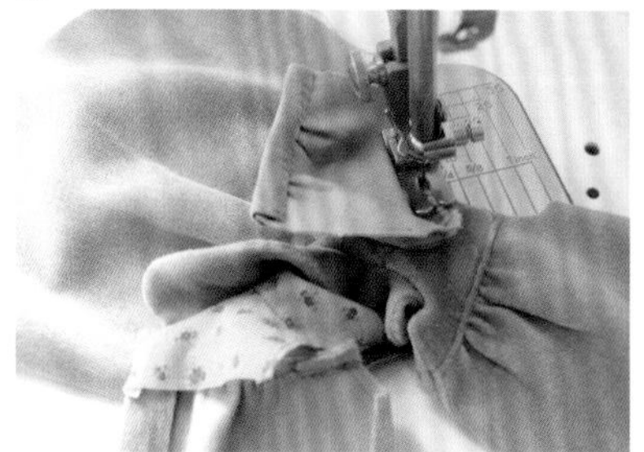

With right sides facing, sew the bodice section and the sleeves together. Raise the machine presser foot a number of times while sewing to gradually align the seam allowances of the sleeve caps and armholes.

33

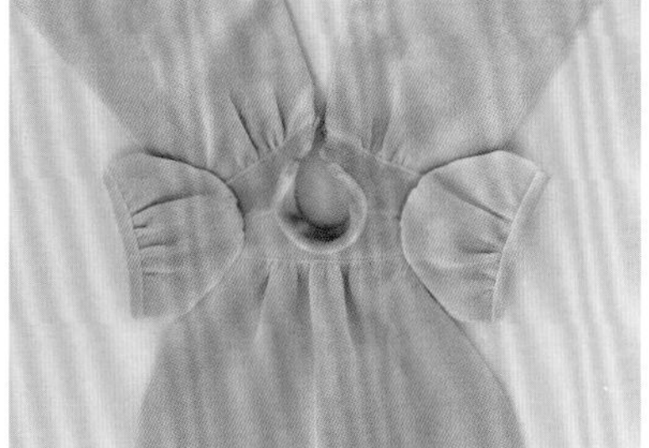

The sleeves are now attached to the bodice. Place the seam allowance toward the sleeves and iron flat.

34

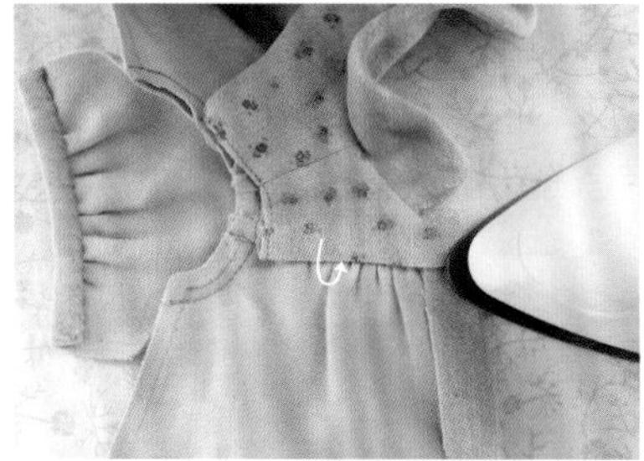

Fold the seam allowance of the front bodice lining inwards and iron flat.

35

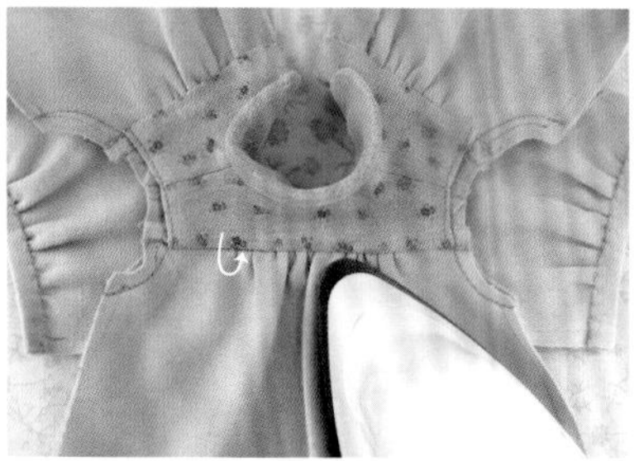

Fold the seam allowance of the back bodice lining inwards and iron flat.

36

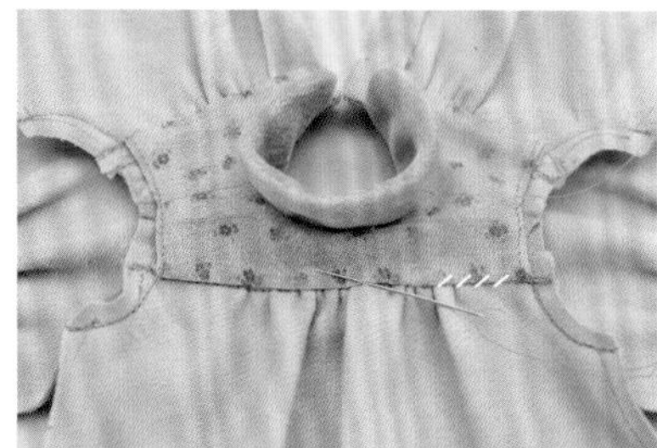

Sew the back bodice lining with blind stitches.

37

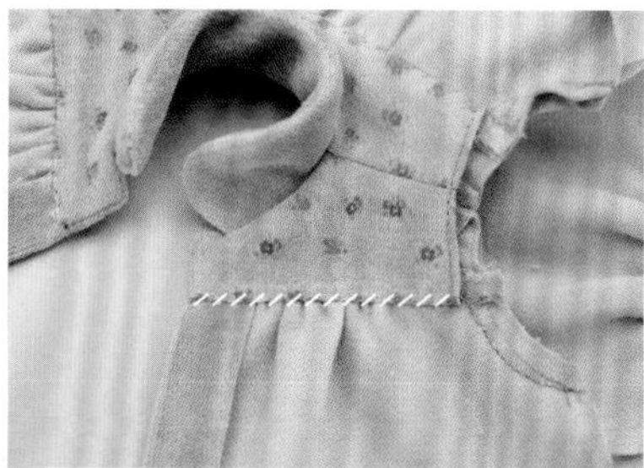

Sew blind stitches on the front bodice lining too.

38

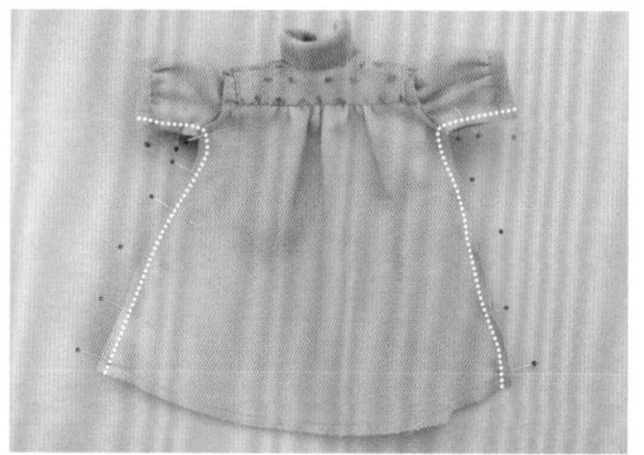

With the right sides of the front and back bodice sections facing, sew them together from the sleeve openings along under the arms and down to the hem.

39

Cut slits into the seam allowance under the arms.

40

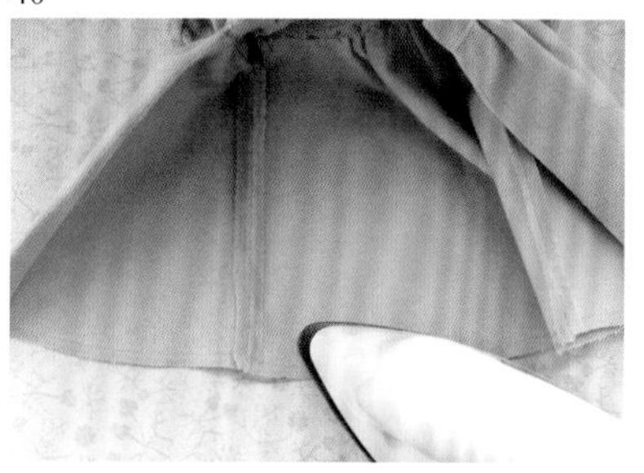

Turn the piece the right side out and iron open the seam allowance.

41

Cut the hem of the seam allowance for the front facing as shown in the picture.

42

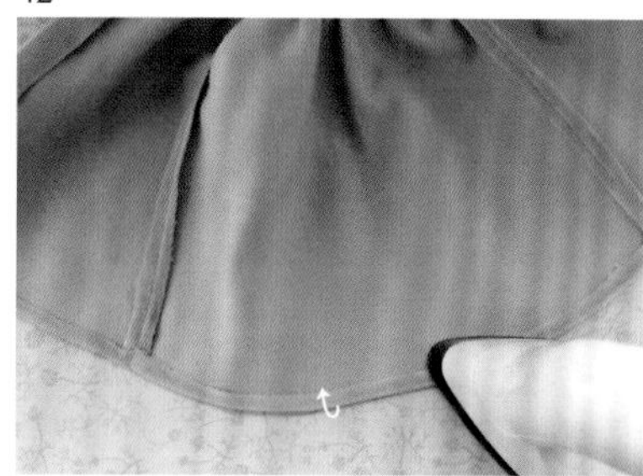

Fold the seam allowance of the hem inward using an iron.

43

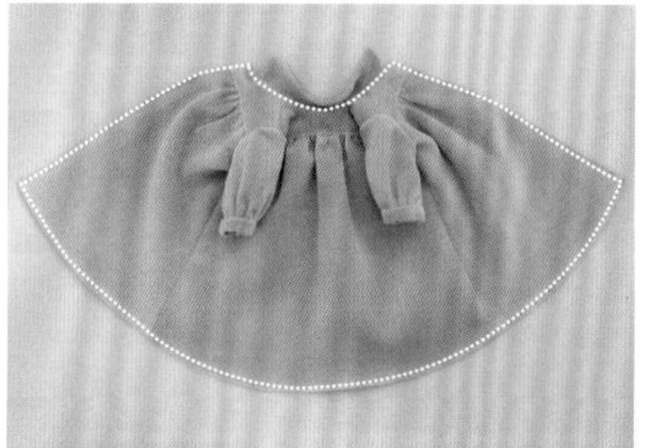

Sew reinforced stitches around the edges from the neckline along the front opening and the hem, then back up to the neckline.

44

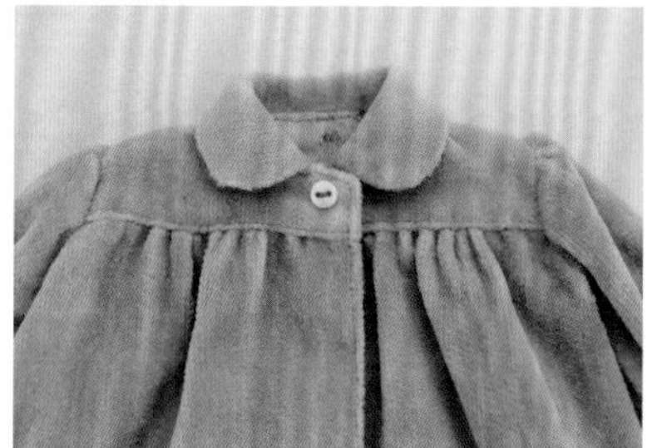

To complete the piece, add decorative buttons. (*For size L, add snaps and decorative buttons to the sleeve openings.)

45

Attach a hook on the front opening and create a loop with thread on the opposite side (refer to p. 93) to complete the piece.

# Shoulder Bag

This simple accessory gives a real sense of being out and about.
Choose a soft, thin leather that is easier to sew.

| | | |
|---|---|---|
| Leather for the bag | S | 5 × 4 cm (2 × 1.6 in) |
| | M | 8 × 6 cm (3.1 × 2.4 in) |
| | L | 10 × 7 cm (3.9 × 2.8 in) |
| 4 mm (0.16 in) jump rings | | 2 pieces |
| Leather for the shoulder strap | S | 0.3 × 15.5 cm (0.12 × 6.1 in) |
| | M | 0.3 × 19 cm (0.12 × 7.5 in) |
| | L | 0.3 × 32 cm (0.12 × 12.6 in) |

1

Arrange the templates on the leather and cut out the sections. Fold the bag section so the right sides are facing and sew both edges. If you use a machine to sew them, place thin paper underneath and sew them together.

2

Backstitch at the beginning and end of the sewing and tie the ends of the thread together.

3

Turn the right side out.

4

Apply leather glue to the top flap.

5

Attach the top flap to the back of the bag.

6

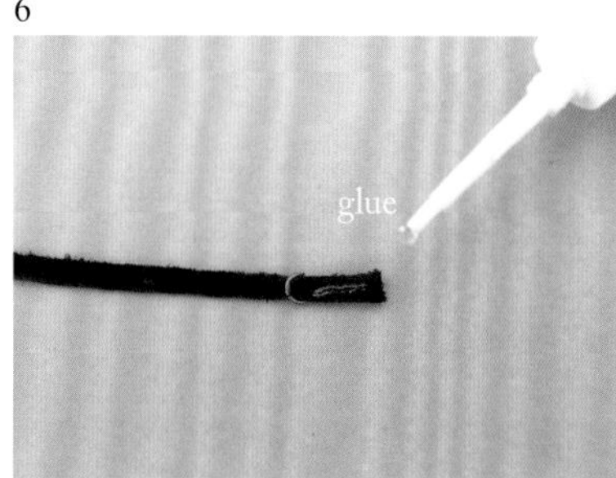


Thread 4 mm (0.16 in) jump rings on to the leather cut for the shoulder strap and add glue to the first 1 cm (0.4 in) of the straps.

7

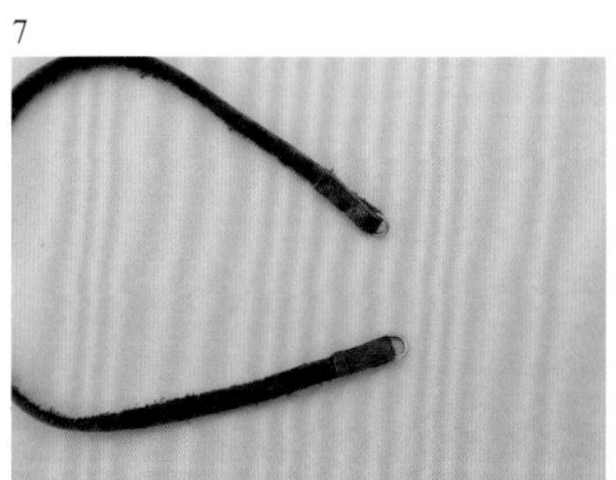

Fold the strap ends over to glue in place and let them dry.

8

Sew the jump rings to the bag.

9

The completed shoulder bag.

# Boots & Socks

Stylish from tip to toe.
Try making them in a whole range of colors.

| | | | |
|---|---|---|---|
| Thin leather in two colors | S 5 × 8 cm (2 × 3.1 in) each<br>M 5.5 × 9 cm (2.2 × 3.5 in) each<br>L 20 × 13 cm (7.9 × 5.1 in) each | Cotton lawn for the insoles | S 3 × 2.5 cm (1.2 × 1 in)<br>M 3 × 3 cm (1.2 × 1.2 in)<br>L 7 × 7.5 cm (2.8 × 3 in) |
| Thick leather for the soles | S 5 × 3 cm (2 × 1.2 in)<br>M 6 × 4 cm (2.4 × 1.6 in)<br>L 11 × 7 cm (4.3 × 2.8 in) | Rib knit for the socks | S 8 × 8 cm (3.1 × 3.1 in)<br>M 10 × 10 cm (3.9 × 3.9 in)<br>L 20 × 20 cm (7.9 × 7.9 in) |
| Silk ribbons | S, M 60 cm (23.6 in)<br>L 80 cm (31.5 in) | Thick paper, double-sided tape, 1.5 mm (0.06 in) hole punch, pounding board, hammer | |

1 

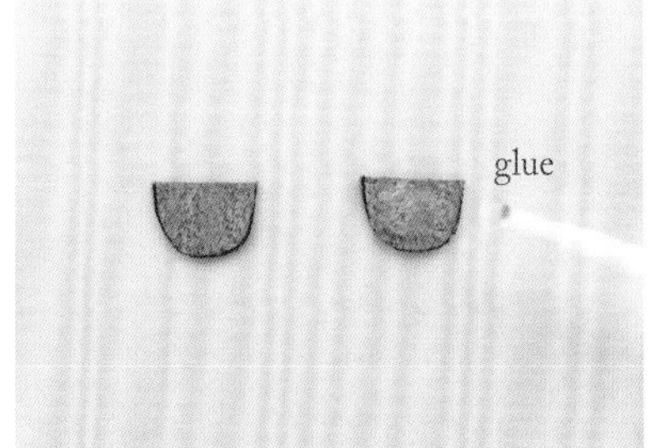


Layer the heel sections cut from the sole leather, fixing them together with leather glue.

2 

For sizes S and M layer two pieces and for size L layer four pieces.

3

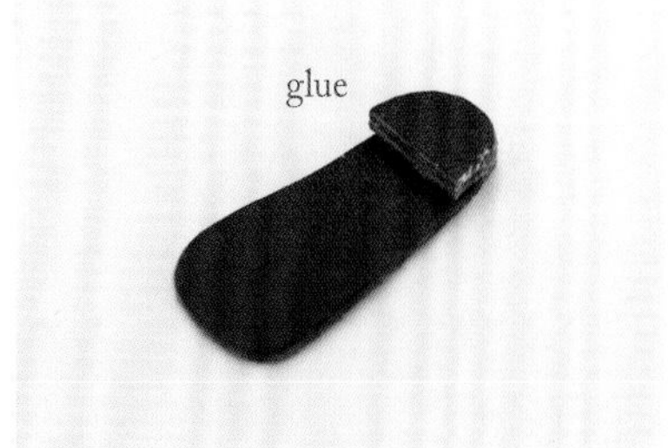


Place the heels on the soles and attach with leather glue.

4

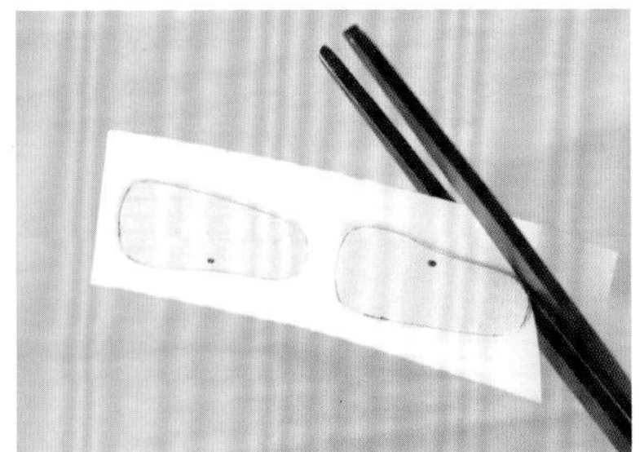

Trace the sole templates on to thick paper to make the insoles, then stick double-sided tape to the front side of the insoles and cut around them.

5

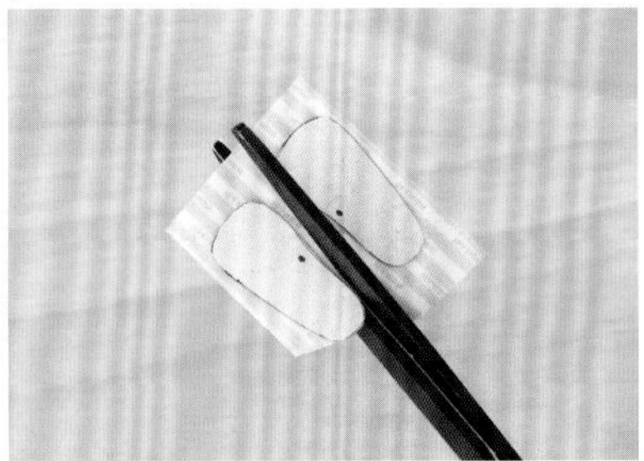

Remove the backing paper from the tape and attach the insoles to the insole fabric.

6

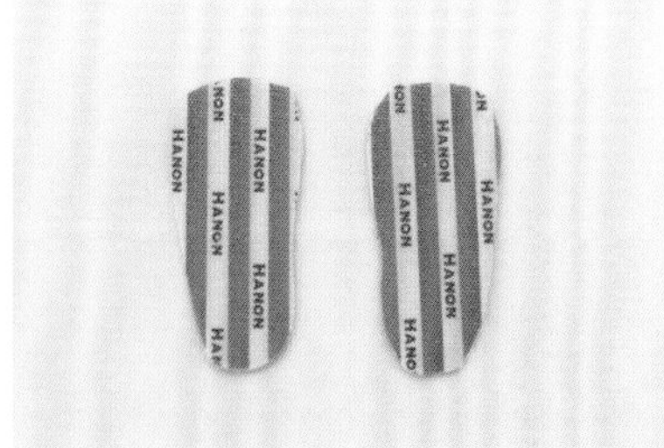

Cut the fabric for the insoles.

7

Attach double-sided tape to the back of the insoles as well, then cut around them.

8

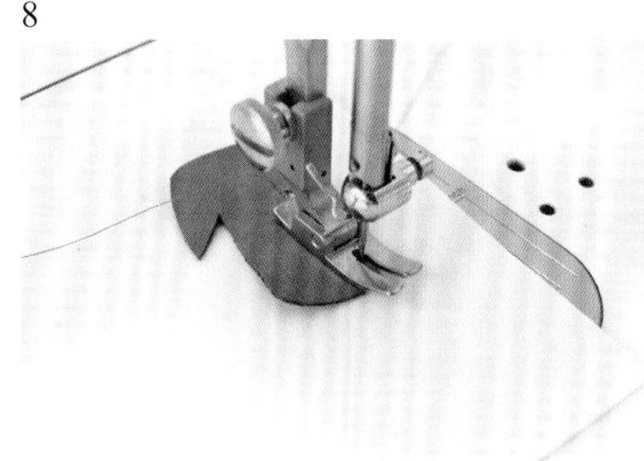

Add decorative stitching around the Part A tongue. If you use a machine to sew the stitches, place thin paper underneath and sew them together.

9 

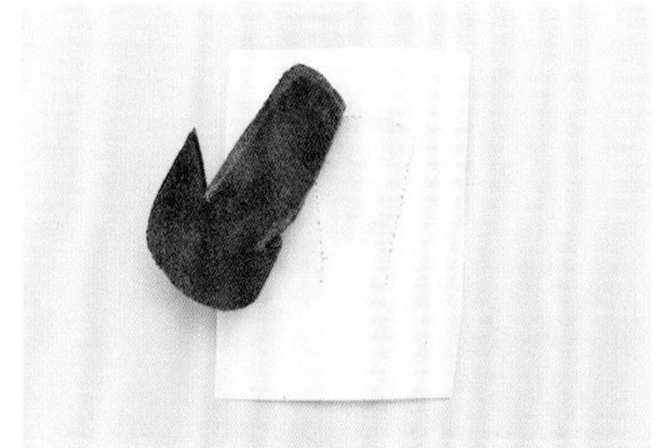

Tie the ends of the threads and remove the paper.

10

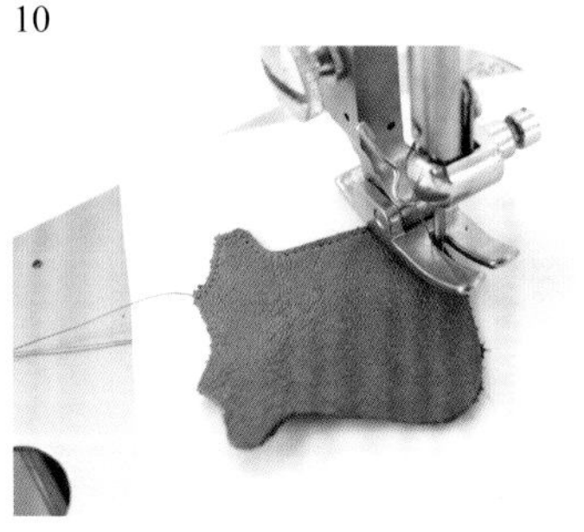

Add decorative stitching around the Part B shaft as well.

11

Tie the ends of the threads and remove the paper.

12

Make holes in Part B. Prepare a 1.5 mm (0.06 in) punch, a pounding board, and a hammer (a tailor's awl can be used instead of a punch to open the holes).

13

Draft the holes so that they match on the left and right, then position the punch vertically on the leather and hit it with the hammer.

14

Make four holes on each side.

15

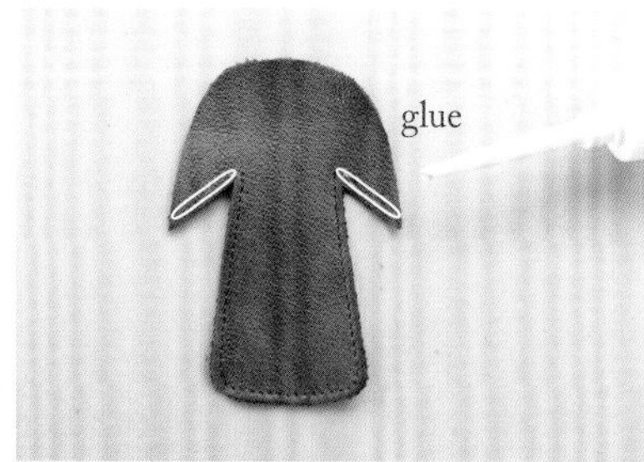


Apply leather glue to the front of Part A as shown in the picture.

16

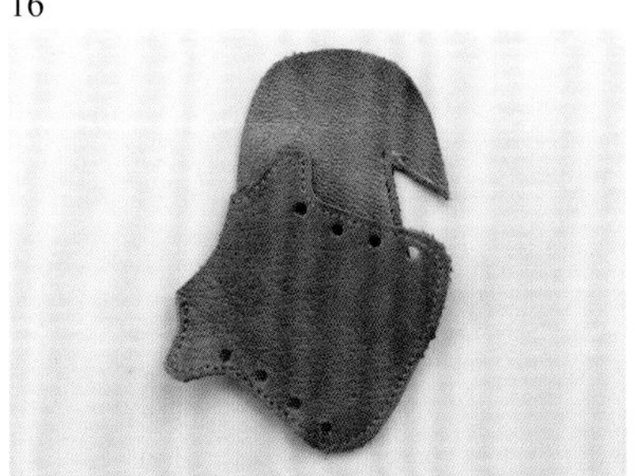

Attach the edge of the Part B shaft to the glue on Part A layering it over by 2 mm (0.08 in) [for size L, layer over by 3 mm (0.12 in)].

17

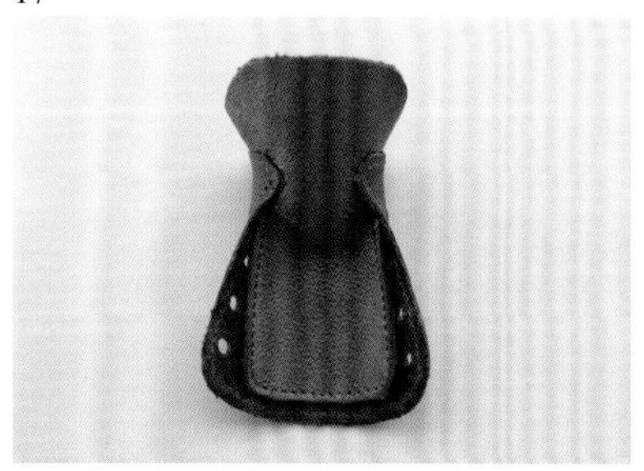

Layer over and attach the pieces in the same way on the other side and dry until they are well bonded.

18

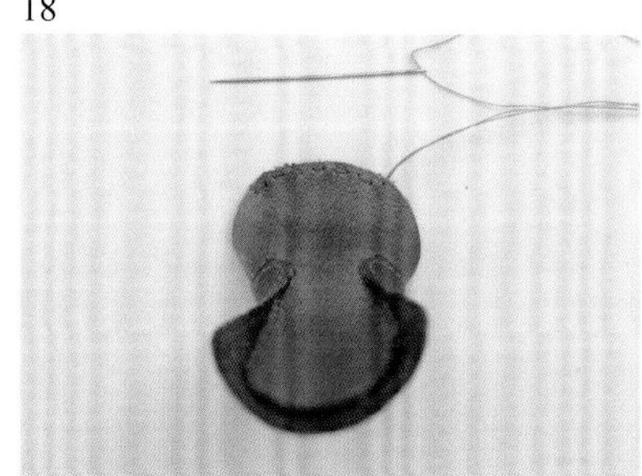

Sew running stitches in the toe of Part A.

19

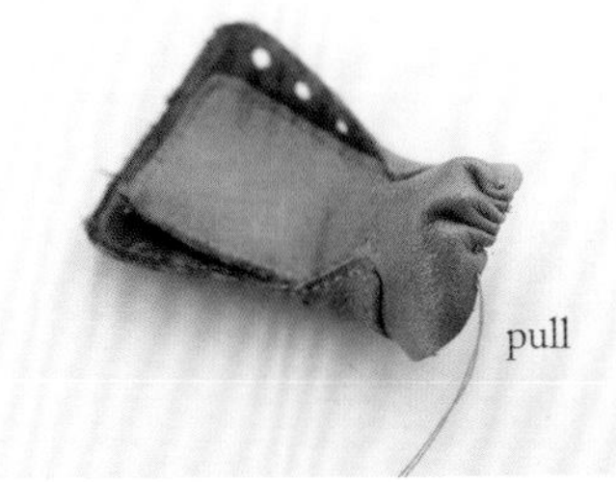


Pull the running stitches to gather the fabric and form the curve of the toe.

20

Remove the backing paper from the tape on the insole backs and insert them into the bottom so the parts wrap around.

21

Fold the leather inward over the insoles and apply leather glue to the bottom.

22

Attach the soles.

23

Dry until well-bonded, then shape.

24

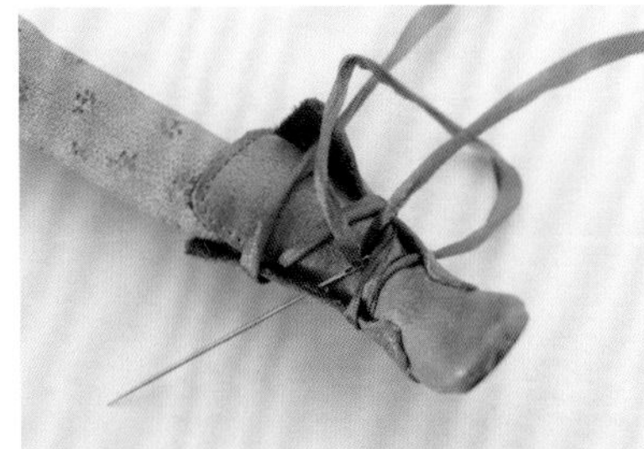

Put the shoes on the doll's feet and lace them up with ribbon to complete the look.

25

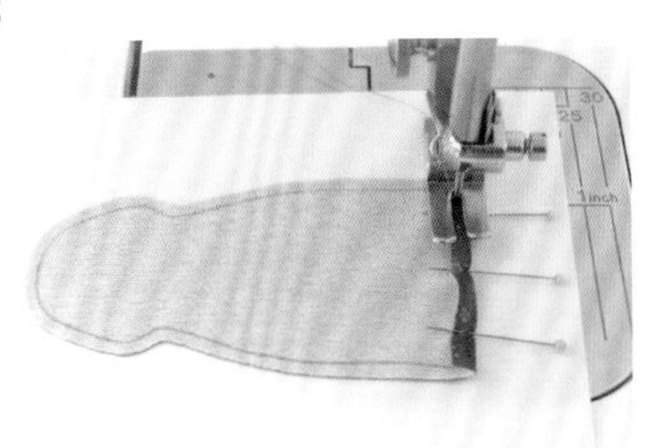

For the knit fabric socks, if you place thin paper underneath when sewing, it creates a clean finish. Fold the sock opening inwards and sew with thread that can be used on knit fabric.

26

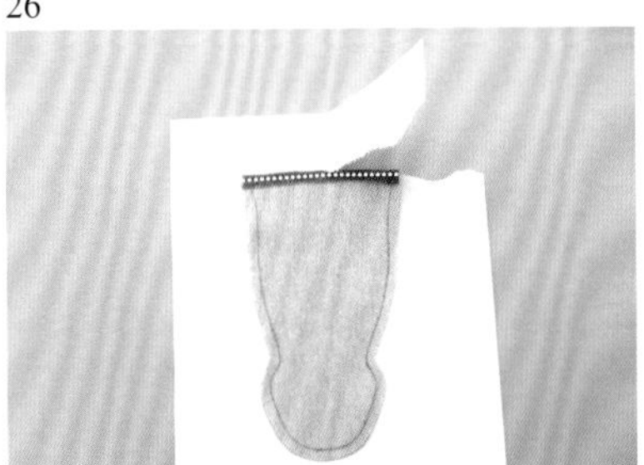

Remove the paper from the fabric after sewing.

27

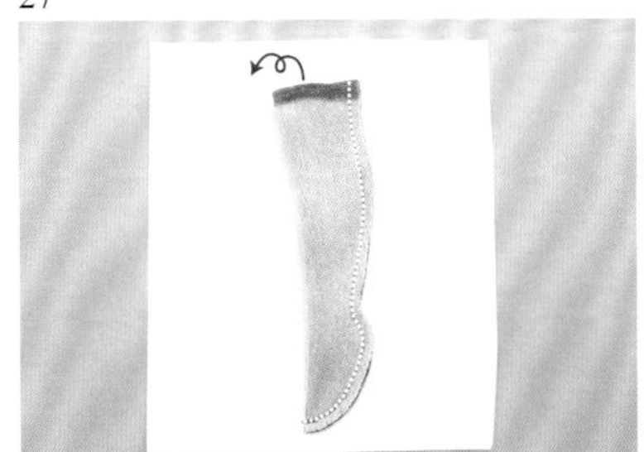

Fold the fabric so the right sides are facing, place paper underneath and sew together. Remove the paper and turn the socks the right side out to complete them.

# Cheeky Fox

What better companion than this cheeky fox?
His mischievous look will warm your heart.

| | |
|---|---|
| Mohair fur | Little brother (Solo) 15 × 10 cm (5.9 × 3.9 in)<br>Big brother (Renard) 15 × 11 cm (5.9 × 4.3 in) |
| Cotton embroidery floss | Black, red |

Insect pins, acrylic paint, cotton stuffing

1

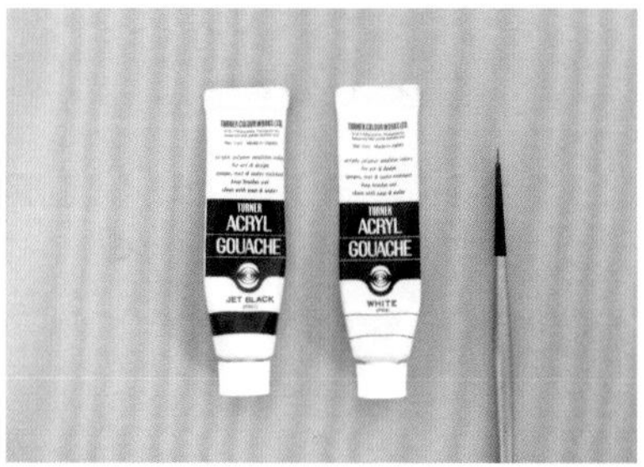


Start by making the eyes. Prepare black and white acrylic paint and a brush.

2

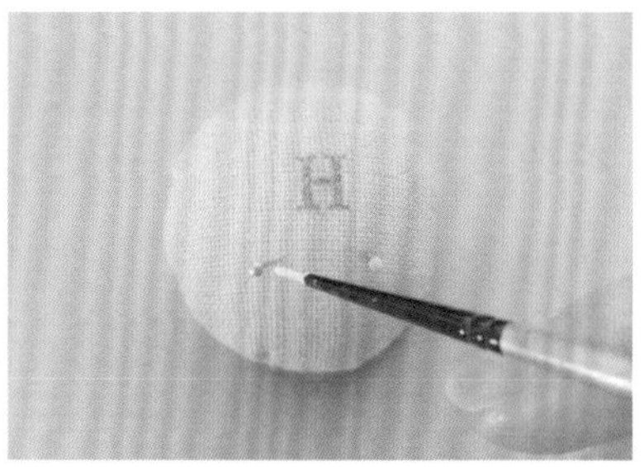

Take two insect pins and paint the pin heads white.

3

Once the white paint has dried, add black dots.

4

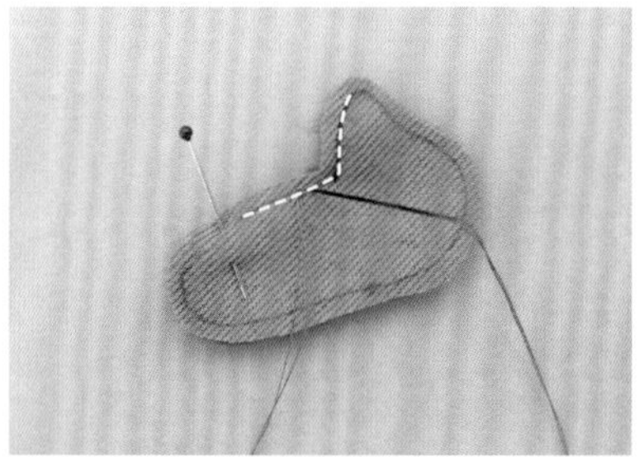

Use the templates to trace the parts on the fabric, taking care to follow the weave, and cut them out. With the right sides of the body section parts facing, backstitch them together from the nose to the tummy opening.

5

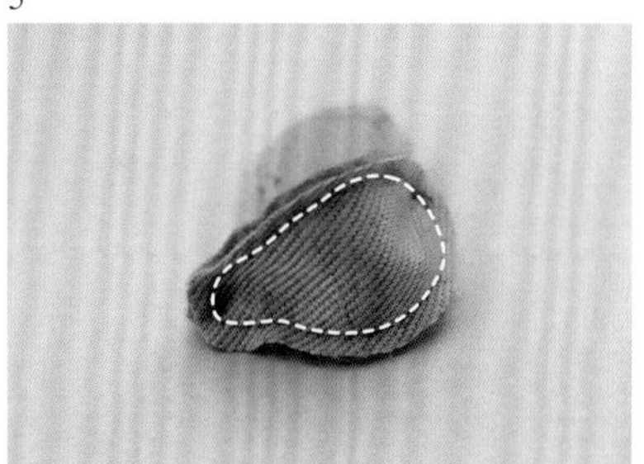

Insert the head into the body section, matching the markers, and with right sides facing, sew from the nose to the back of the head.

6

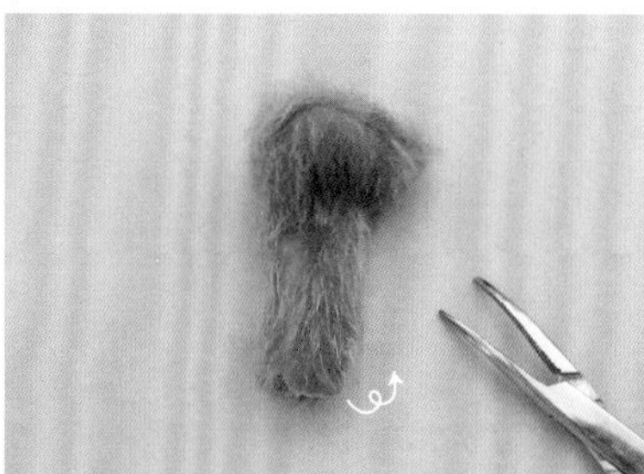

Sew from the back of the head to the opening as well with right sides facing. Then cut slits into the seam allowance and turn the right side out from the bottom opening.

7

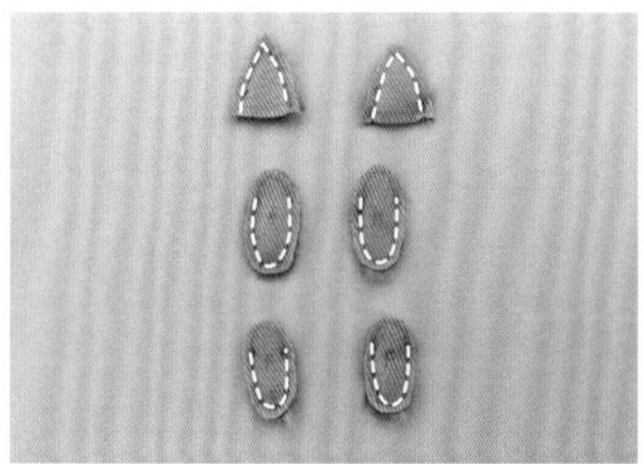

With the right sides facing, sew the ears, front paws, and legs, leaving openings.

8

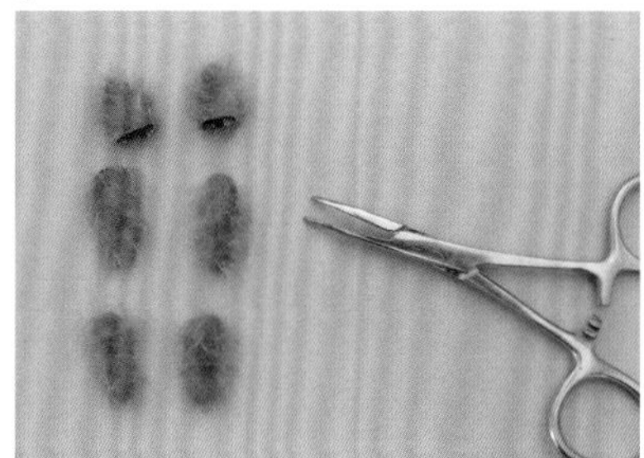

Cut the corners of the ears' seam allowance, then cut fine slits into the seam allowance of the front paws and legs, and turn the right side out.

9

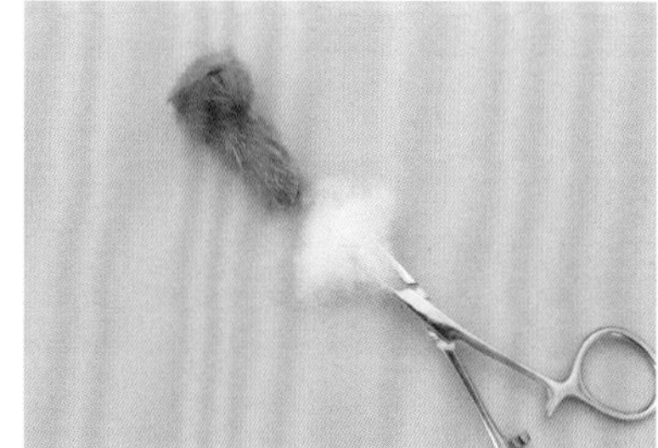

Stuff the body.

10

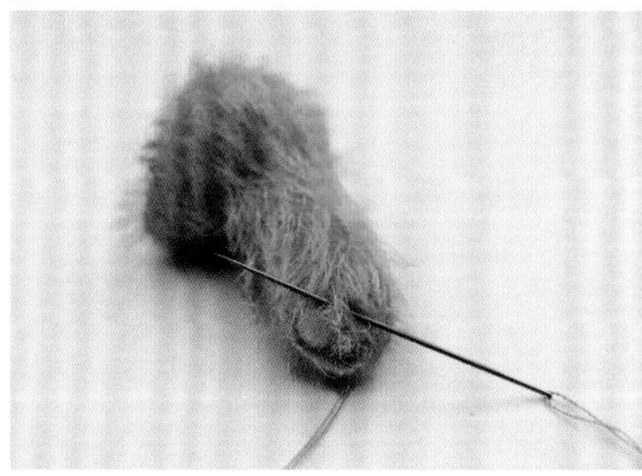

Sew the openings using ladder stitch. Stuff the front paws and legs too, then sew the openings closed.

11

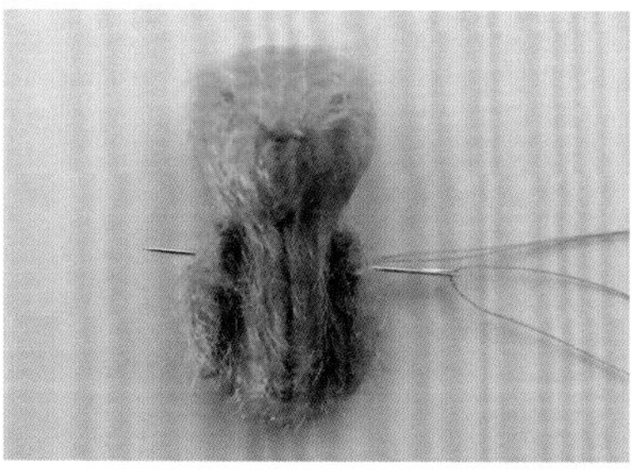

Attach the front paws to the body. Sew by passing the needle through repeatedly so the thread stays at one point.

12

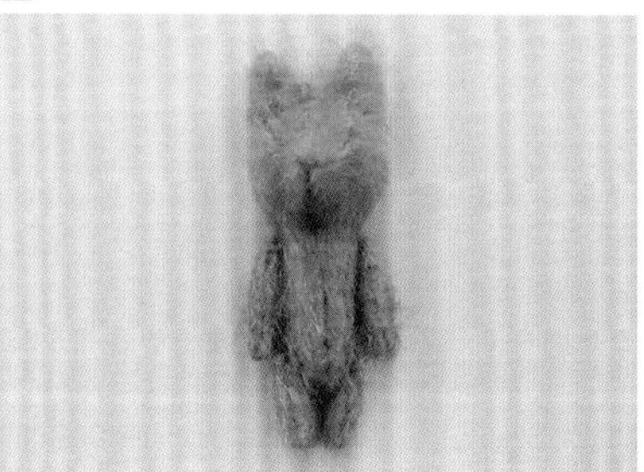

Sew the legs on in the same way and so that they can move.

13

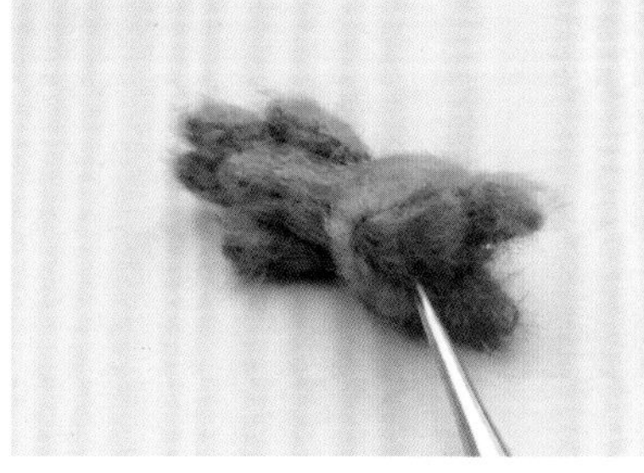

Use a tailor's awl to open holes where the eyes will go, apply glue to the heads of the insect pins and insert them.

14

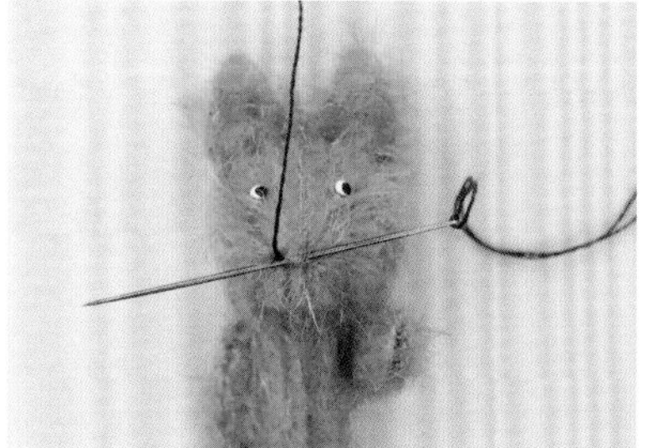

Use one strand of black embroidery floss to sew stitches for the nose.

15

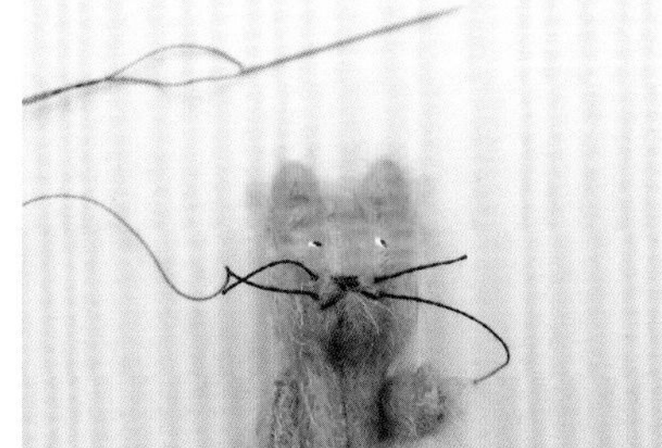

Use embroidery thread to make whiskers. Make a French knot 2 cm (0.8 in) from the tip, then thread the needle through to the other side and make another French knot, then cut the thread to leave short ends.

16

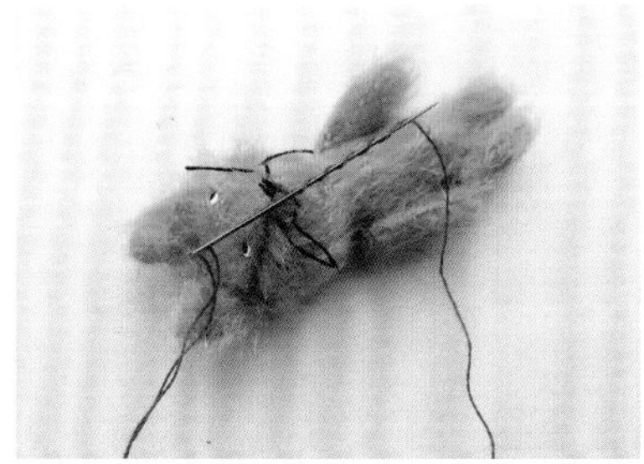

Using a single strand of red embroidery thread, sew into the place where the tongue will go, and wrap the thread five times round the needle.

17

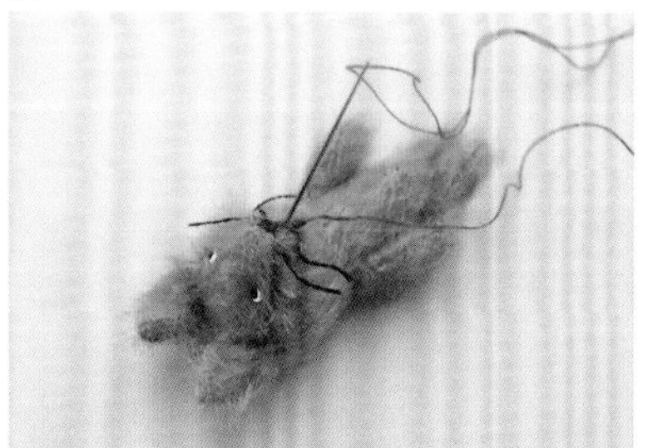

Push the needle back in right next to where it came out and pull the thread to make the tongue.

18

Add a ribbon round the fox's neck for a finishing touch.

# Gather

This is how to make gathering for the skirts, sleeves, and cuffs.

1

Adjust the machine setting so the length of the stitch is 2.5–3 mm (0.1–0.12 in).

2

Sew along the center of the seam allowance without doing reverse stitch at the start and end.

3

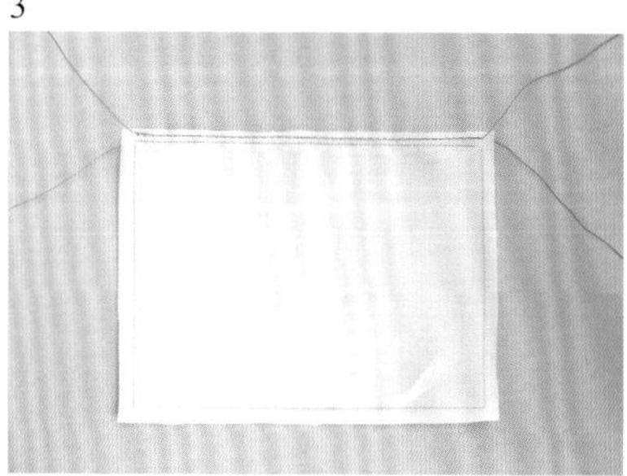

To make it easier to pull the threads, leave ends of about 15 cm (5.9 in) on both sides.

4

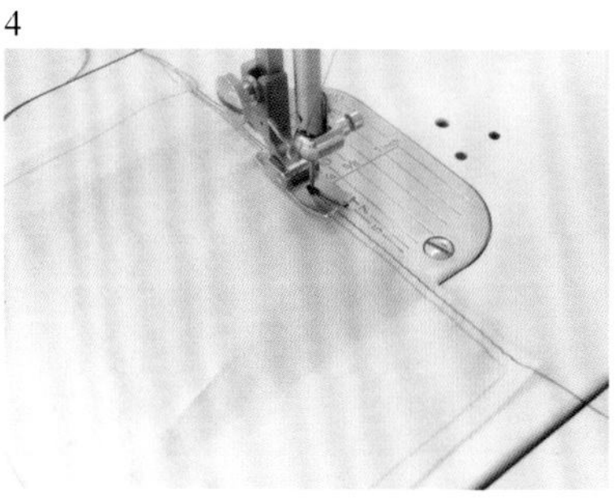

Sew a second line of stitches very close to and running directly parallel to the first line.

5

Separate the top and bottom threads.

6

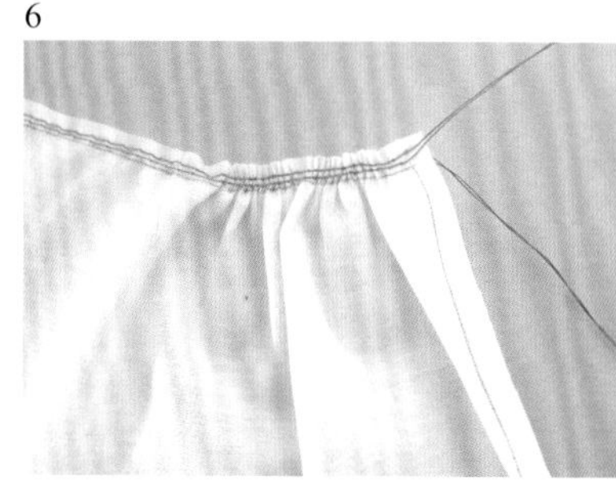

Pull only the two top threads to gather the fabric. If the length of the gathering is long, pull from both sides, and in the case that it is a short length, tie the ends at one side and pull from one side.

7

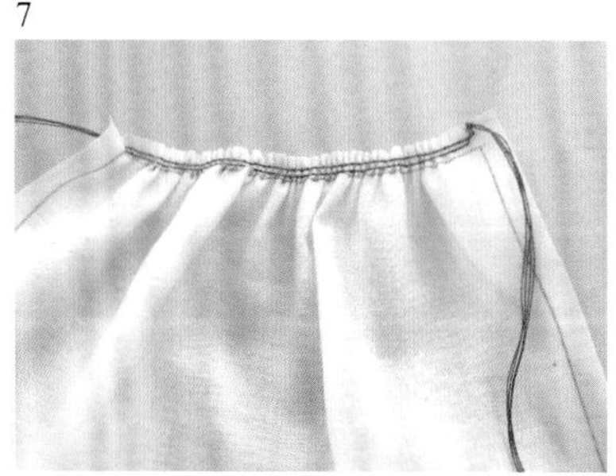

Once it is gathered to the correct length, tie the top threads. Tie the bottom threads in the same way. Do the same on the other side to fix the width of the gathering.

8

Neaten the spacing of the gathering and iron flat.

9

Here the fabric is gathered. The gathering stitches on the seam allowance can be pulled out if desired.

# Thread Loop

This is how to make a thread loop for the front opening of the waistcoat and coat.

1

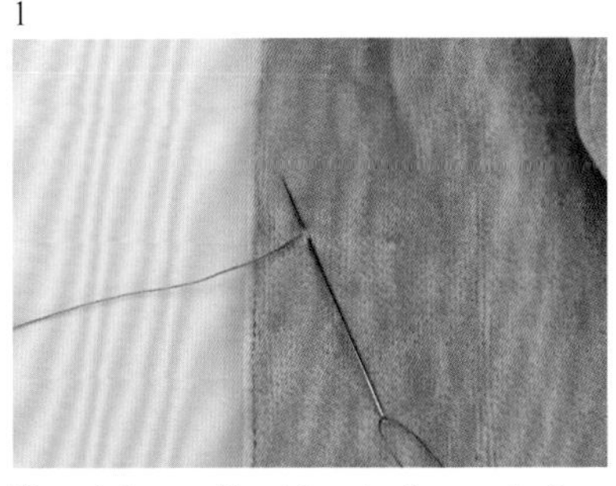

Thread the needle with a single strand of sewing thread. Pass the needle through where the hook will overlap and then slightly catch the fabric right next to where the thread comes out.

2

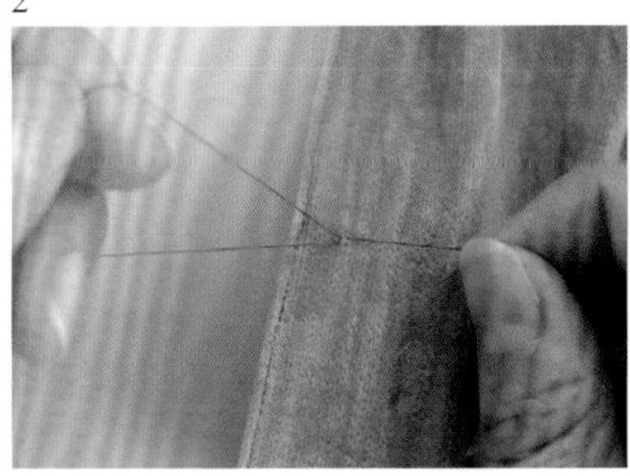

Pull the thread partway through and form a loop as shown in the picture. From here on, the loop is worked with the fingers.

3

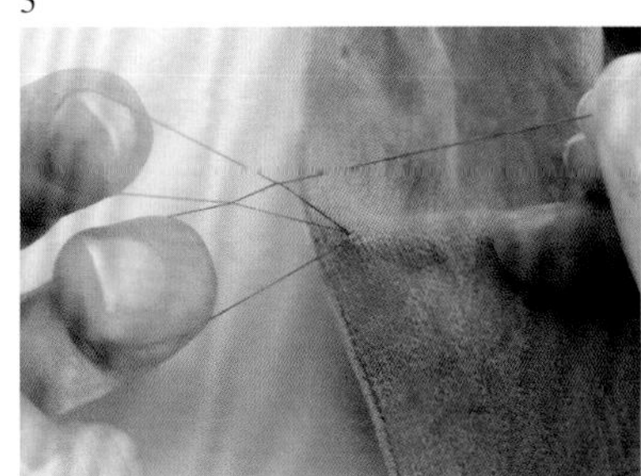

Loop over the thread in your right hand to create a new loop.

4

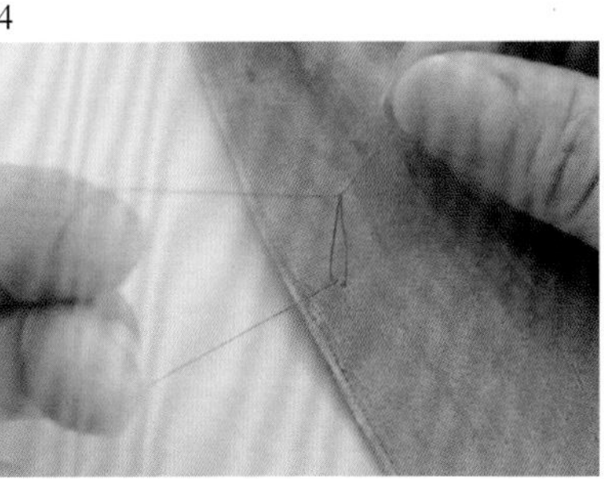

Pull the thread and tighten to make the created loop smaller.

5

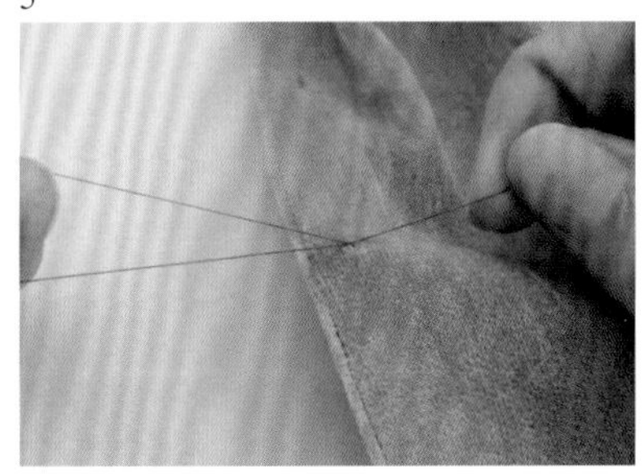

Here one chain loop has been completed. Loop over the thread in your right hand on to the new loop and keep repeating to create more chain loops.

6

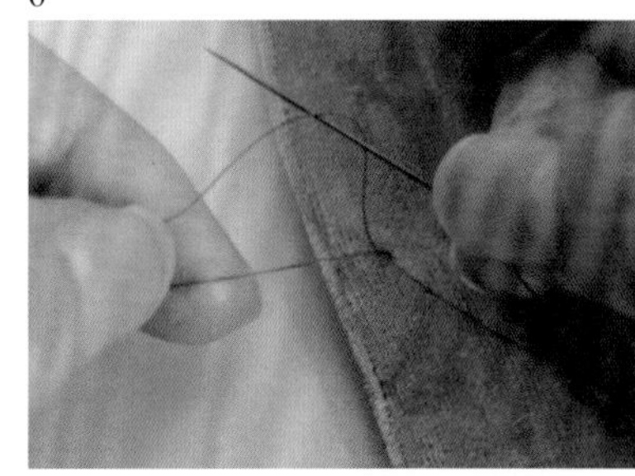

Once the chain loops are slightly longer than the width of the hook, pass the thread right through the loop.

7

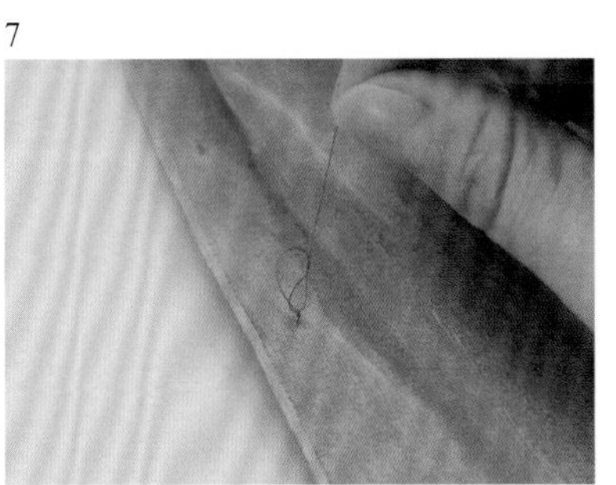

Pull the thread to tighten the loop.

8

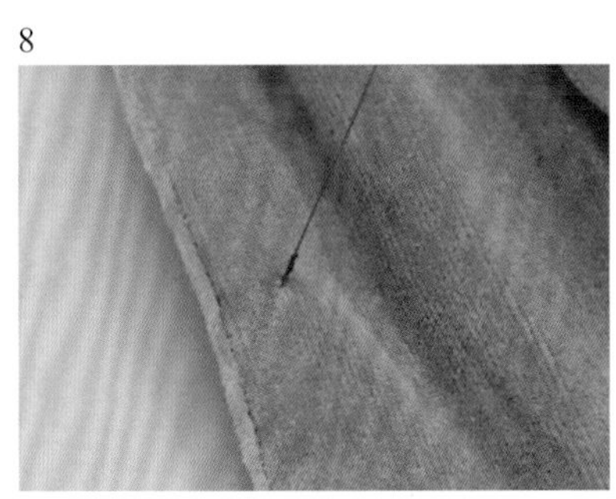

Here the chain loops are fastened.

9

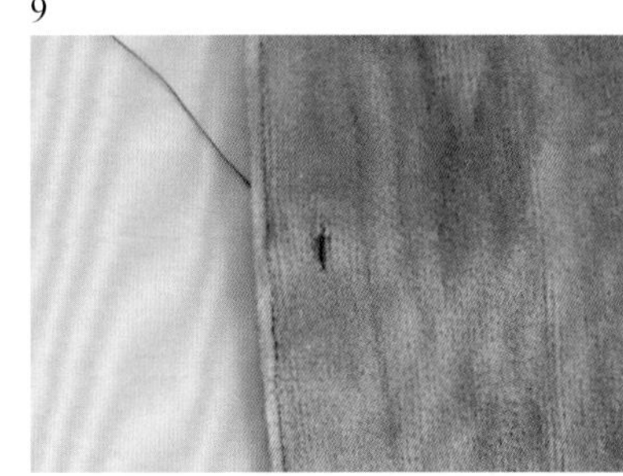

Sew the chain looped thread parallel to the opening and fix with a French knot to complete the thread loop.

Model Dolls:

b.m.b.Cherry

be by baby! Cherry ©miyuking INC.JAPAN

Tiny Betsy McCall



U-noa Quluts Light



U-noa Quluts Girl

Photography: Takanori Katsura, Asako Tanaka (uNdercurrent)

Styling: Rieko Ohashi

Digital Tracing: Yukari Kyusuke

Photography Support: kinoe-ne (Miniature Hangers), coeur lapin (Glass Eyes)

Editing: Yoko Suzuki

Design: Asako Tanaka (uNdercurrent)

Support: MIYUKING, Renkinjyutsu-Koubou, Inc. (Alchemic Labo), Sekiguchi Co., Ltd

Translation: Wendy Uchimura
Thanks to TIME & SPACE, INC. for help with translation
http://www.timeandspace.jp

Author: Satomi Fujii

Publisher: Daisuke Matsushita

*Doll Sewing Book HANON*

Original Japanese edition is published by Hobby Japan Co., Ltd.

English edition published in 2019 by:
NIPPAN IPS Co., Ltd.
1-3-4 Yushima
Bunkyo-ku, Tokyo,
113-0034, Japan

ISBN 978-4-86505-226-8



Printed in China

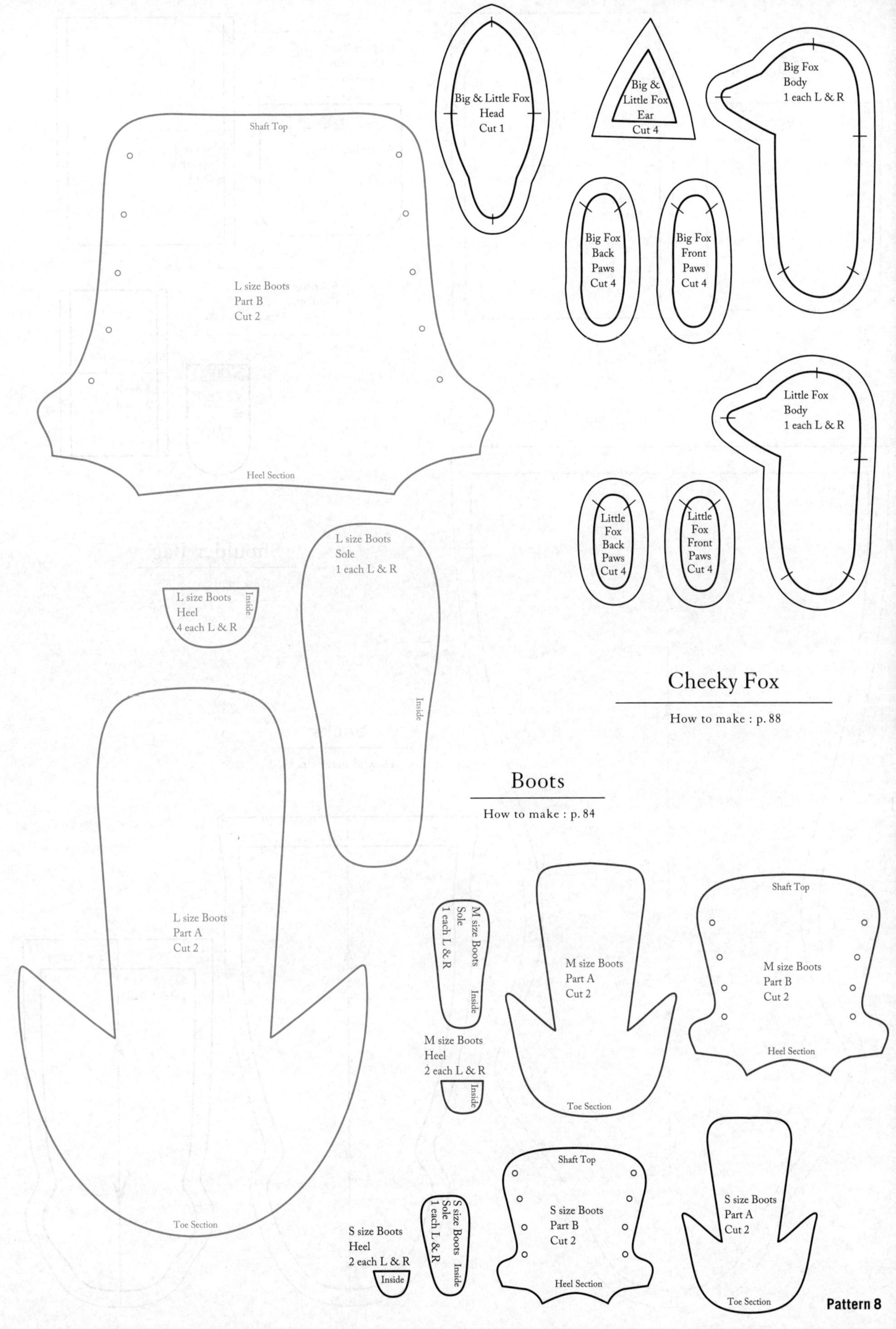


## Cheeky Fox

How to make : p. 88

## Boots

How to make : p. 84

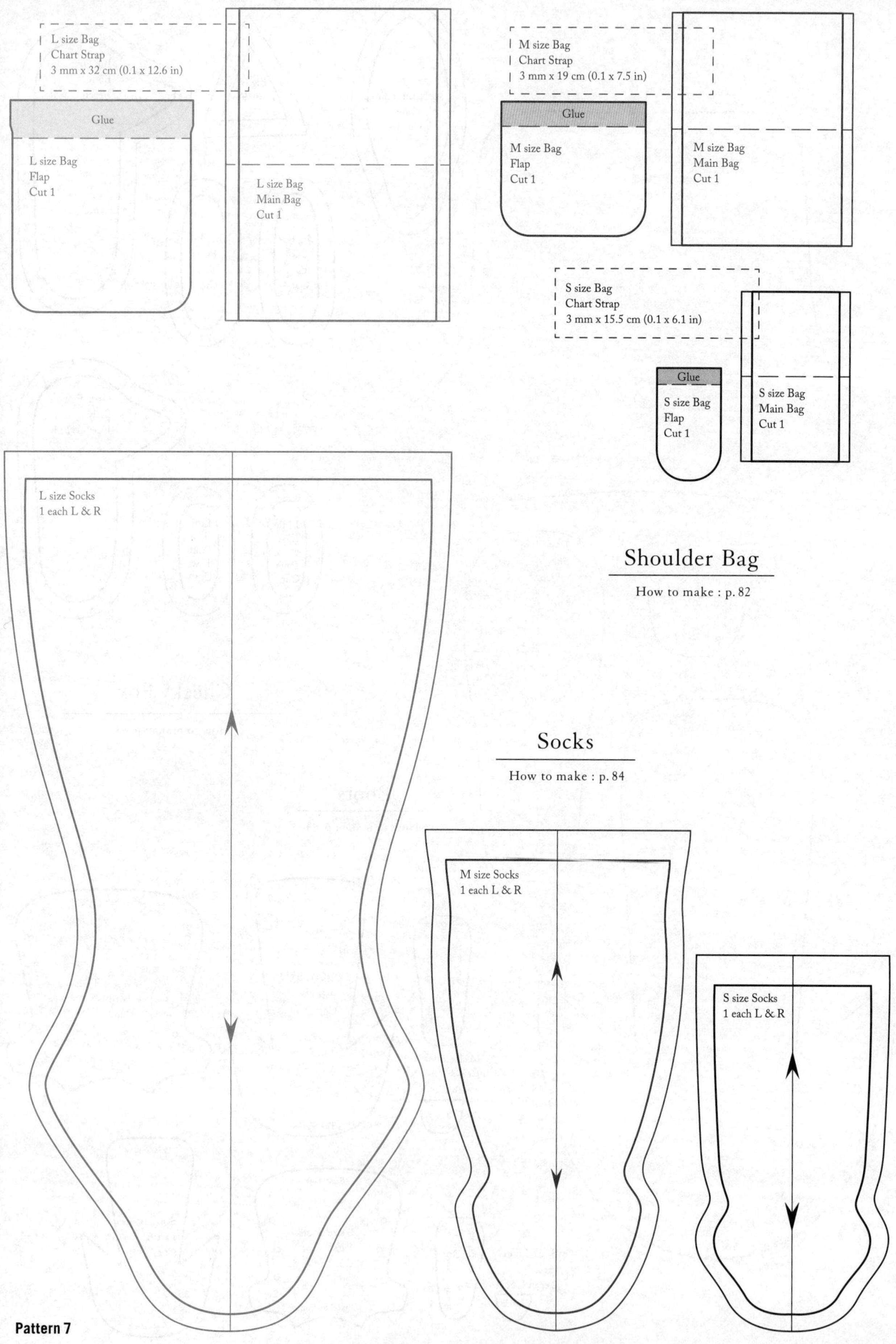


## Shoulder Bag

How to make : p. 82

## Socks

How to make : p. 84

# Waistcoat

How to make : p. 68

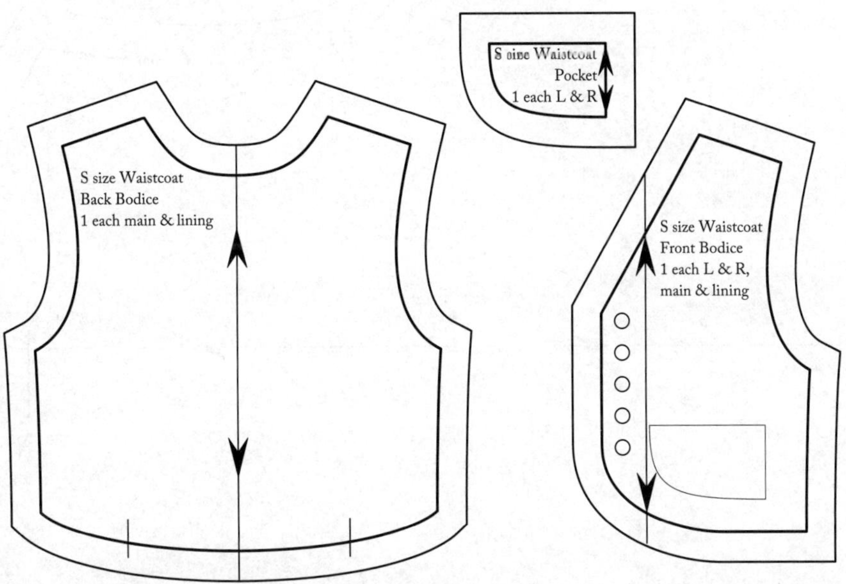


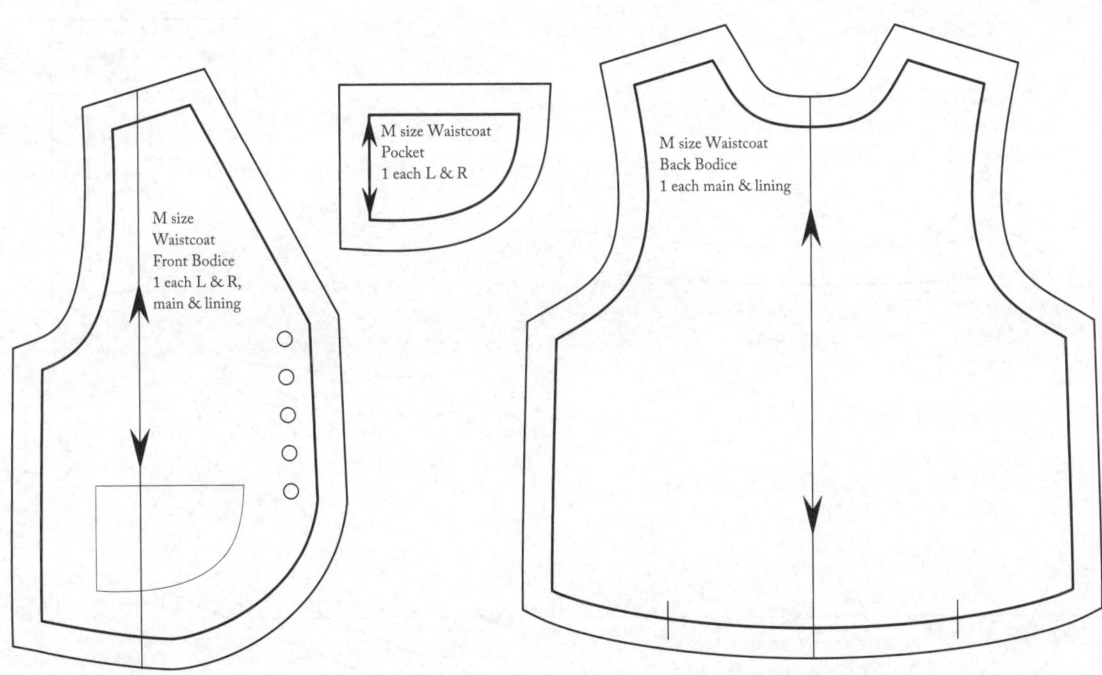

# Waistcoat

How to make : p. 68

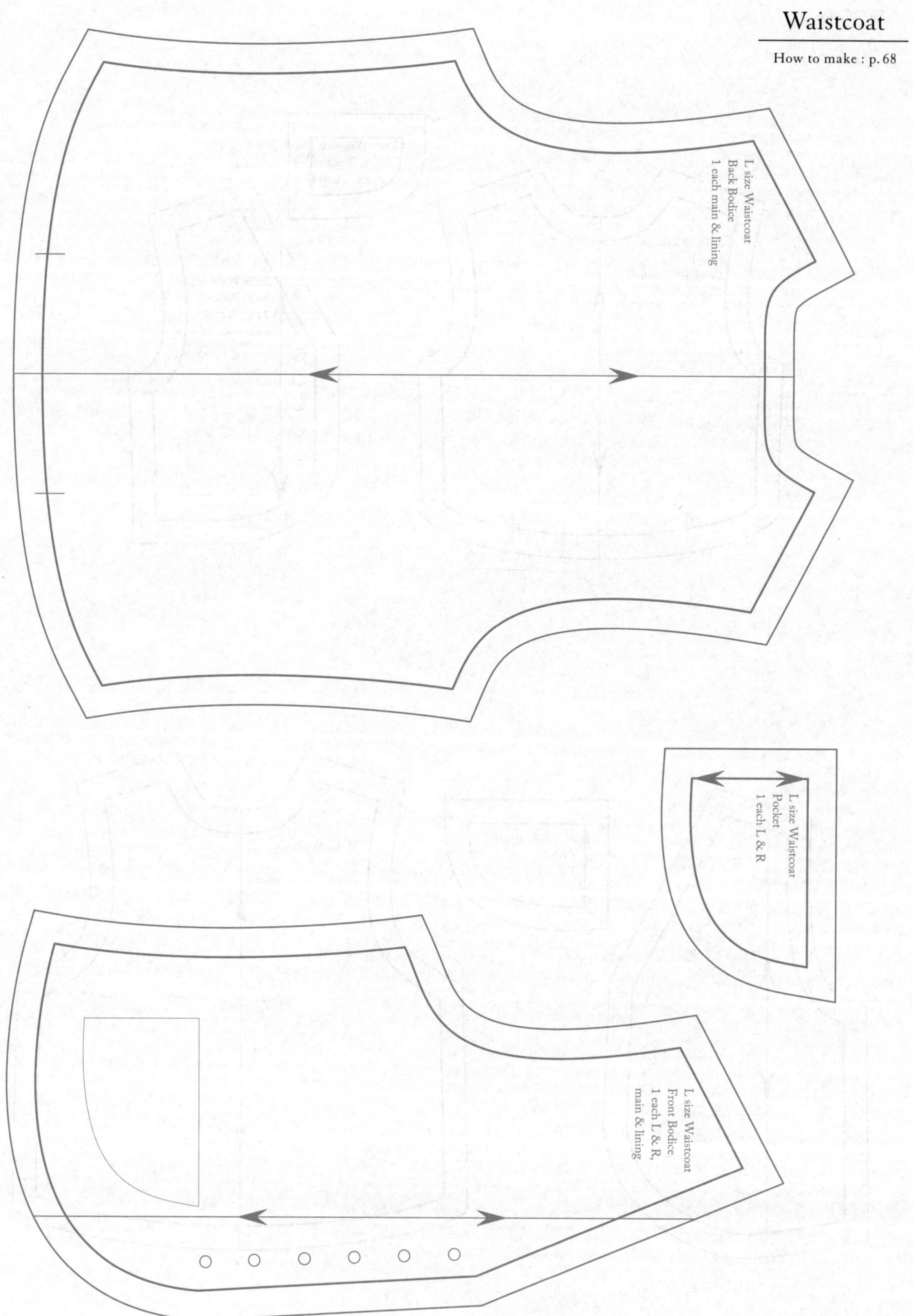

# Waist Apron

How to make : p. 48

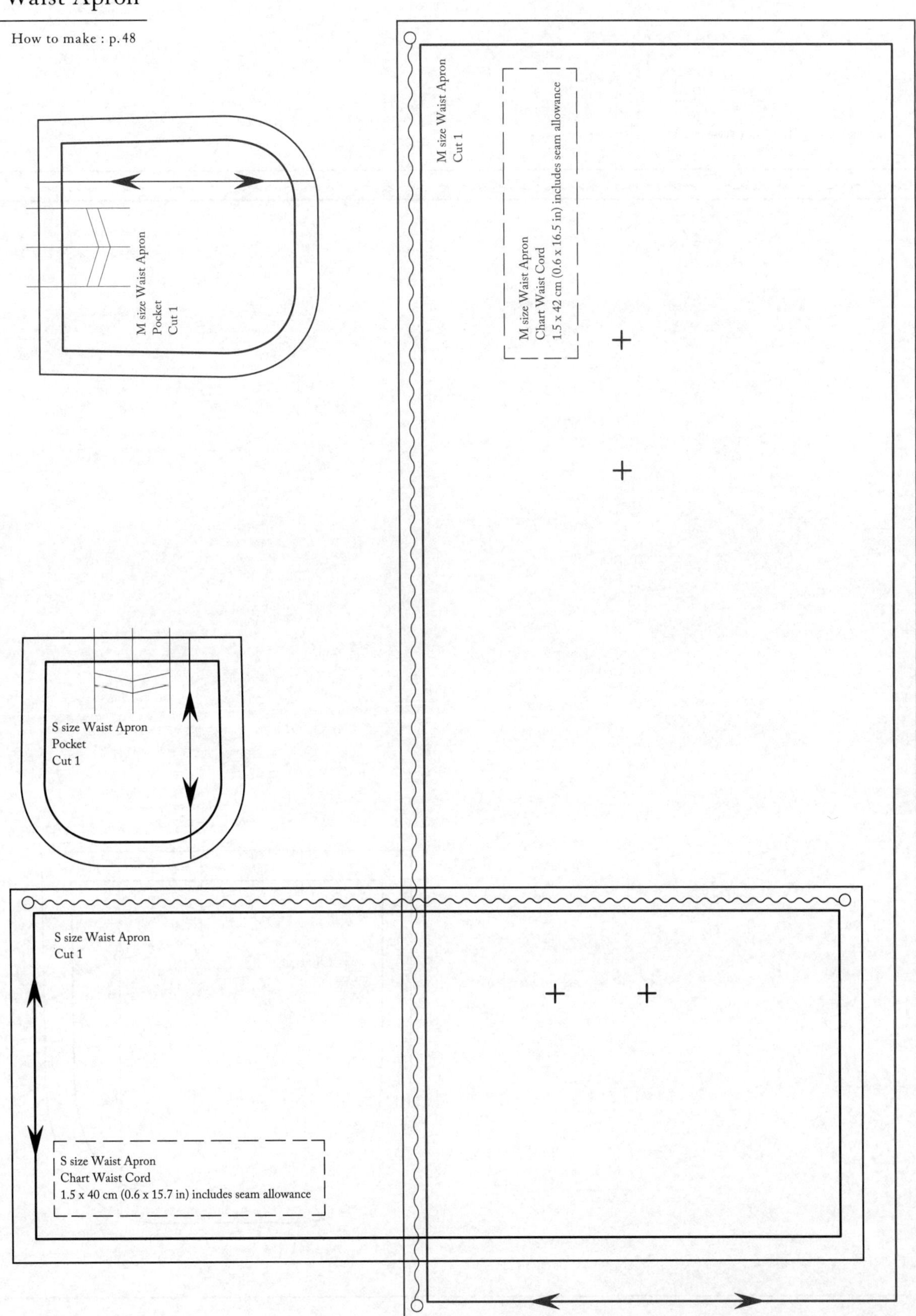

# Waist Apron

How to make : p.48

L size Waist Apron
Chart Waist Cord
2 x 72 cm (0.8 x 28 in) includes seam allowance

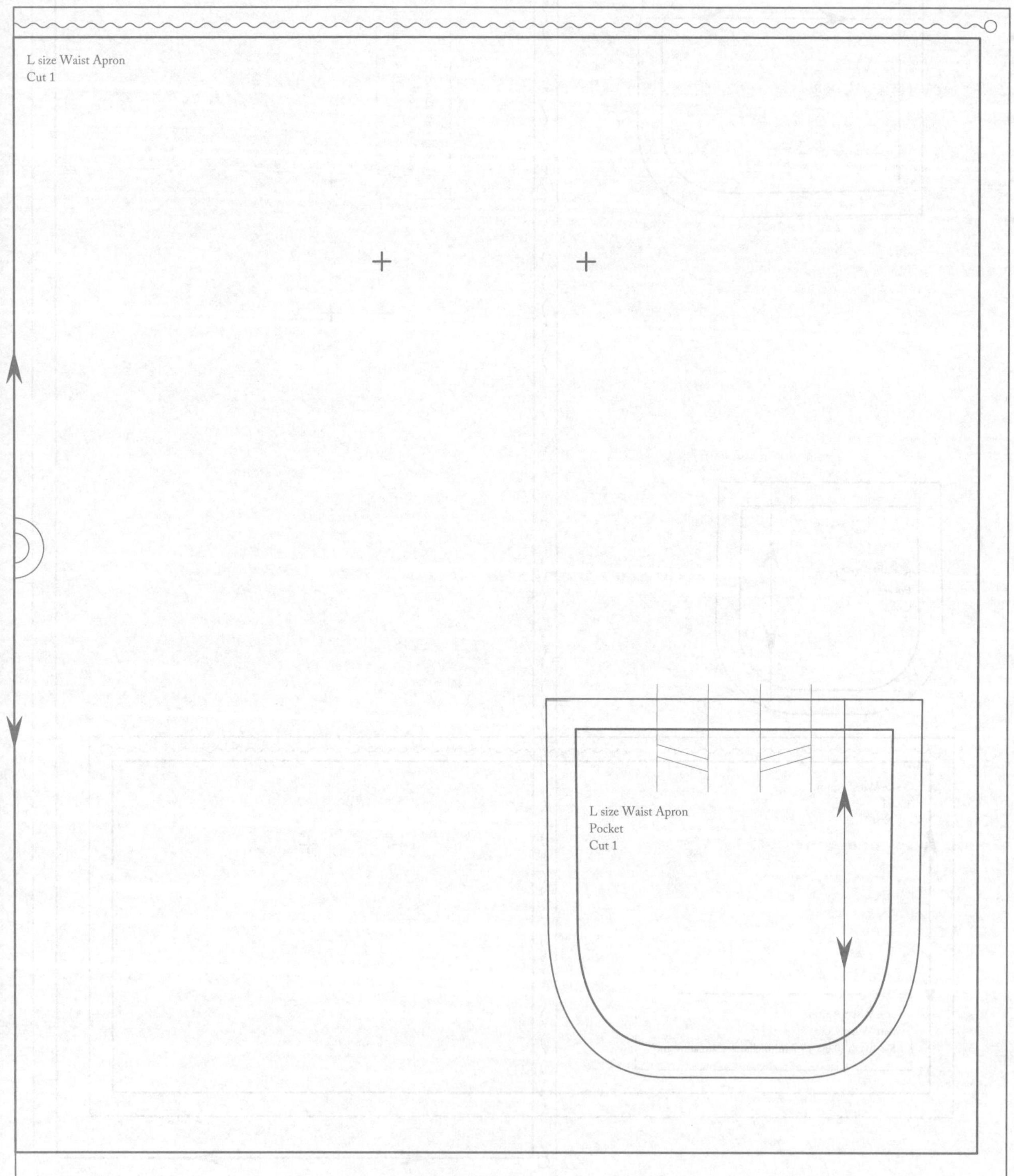

## Lace Strap Dress

How to make : p. 36

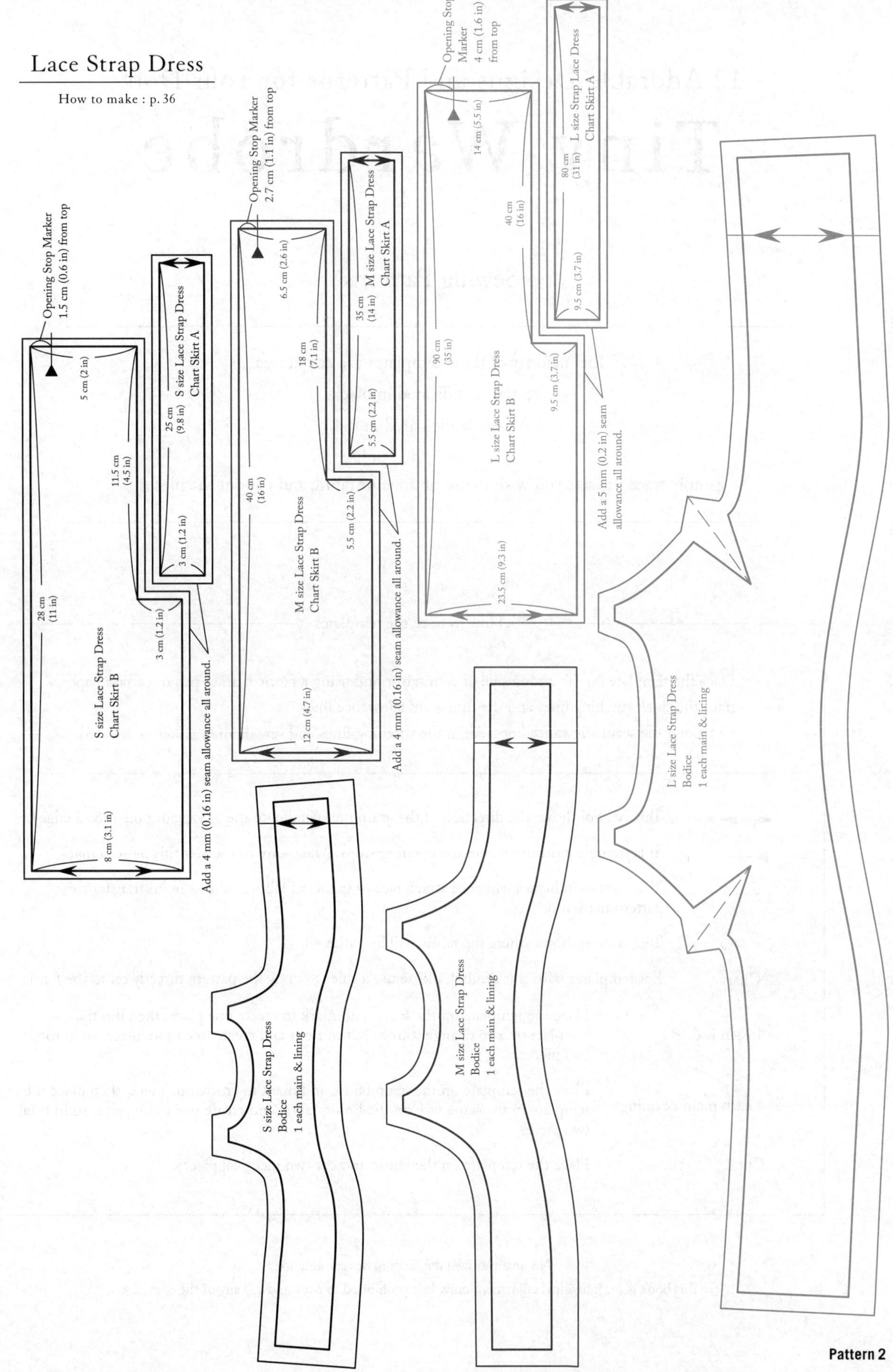

12 Adorable Designs and Patterns for Your Doll

# Tiny Wardrobe

## Sewing Patterns

The majority of these templates are actual size.
S size is indicated in black.
M size is indicated in red.
L size is indicated in blue.
Simply trace the size you wish to use on to your fabric and cut out the pieces.

### How to trace the templates

Place the template on the wrong side of your fabric and using a fabric marker pen or carbon paper, trace the thick stitching lines and the thin seam allowance lines.
Cut along the seam allowance lines. Align the stitching lines and sew them together as directed.

|  |  |
|---|---|
| ←→ | This symbol shows the direction of the grainline (parallel to the selvage or non-frayed edge). |
| ▶— | This triangle indicates where the opening stops. Make sure to transfer this pattern mark. |
| — | This symbol indicates where to attach lace or gathered fabric. Make sure to transfer this pattern mark too. |
| o〰o | This symbol shows where the fabric will be gathered. |
| 「Chart」 | For templates with this symbol, please use a ruler to draw the pattern directly on to the fabric. |
| 「1 each L & R」 | Place the template on the fabric and mark to create one piece, then flip the template over to change it from left to right and create one more piece, so in total two pieces. |
| 「1 each main & lining」 | Place the template on the main fabric and mark to create one piece, then place the template in the same way on the lining fabric and create one more piece, so in total two pieces. |
| 「Cut 2」 | Place the template on the fabric and cut two identical pieces. |